HOW TO CRACK AN EGG WITH ONE HAND

HOW TO CRACK AN EGG WITH ONE HAND

A pocket book for the new mother

FRANCESCA BEAUMAN

BLOOMSBURY

LONDON · BERLIN · NEW YORK · SYDNEY

First published in Great Britain 2011

Copyright © 2011 by Francesca Beauman
Illustrations © 2011 by Zoe More O'Ferrall and Holly Macdonald

The moral right of the author has been asserted

Every reasonable effort has been made to trace copyright holders of
material reproduced in this book, but if any have been inadvertently
overlooked the publishers would be glad to hear from them. For legal
purposes the permissions list on pages 214–215 constitutes an
extension of the copyright page.

Bloomsbury Publishing, London, Berlin, New York and Sydney

36 Soho Square, London W1D 3QY

A CIP catalogue record for this book is available from the British Library

ISBN 978 0 7475 9793 3
10 9 8 7 6 5 4 3 2 1

Typeset by Hewer Text UK Ltd, Edinburgh
Printed in Great Britain by Clays Ltd, St Ives Plc

MIX
Paper from
responsible sources
FSC® C018072

www.bloomsbury.com/francescabeauman

CONTENTS

INTRODUCTION

'I am in pig, what d'you think of that?'

'A most hideous expression, Linda dear,' said Aunt Emily, 'but I suppose we must congratulate you.'

'I suppose so,' said Linda. She sank into a chair with an enormous sigh. 'I feel awfully ill, I must say.'

'But think how much good it will do you in the long run,' said Davey, enviously, 'such a wonderful clear-out.'

FROM the day that you, like Linda in *The Pursuit of Love* by Nancy Mitford (1945), announce to the world that you are pregnant, the most intimate parts of your body suddenly become public property, and it becomes seemingly socially acceptable for complete strangers to ask you about the size of your cervix. This is not the only reason why, on paper, the decision to have a baby is a completely irrational one. It drains you of sleep, money, opportunities to wear very high heels and a whole other multitude of pleasures. Yet, for some reason, lots of us still choose to do it, year after year after year. The thing is, if it was about being rational, the human race would have died out before Adam and Eve had even had a chance to shake the mud off their gardening gloves.

The result? Last year in Britain 708,711 babies were born. Simultaneously, almost the same number of books about babies were published. The huge majority of these books were the sort of narrowly focused babycare manuals that, in the twenty-first century, have come to seem increasingly outdated. These days, becoming a new mother is no longer just about learning how to change a nappy or help your baby sleep through the night: rather, it is a dizzying and delicate dance around an endless, wearisome barrage of new products, new advice, new scientific studies and new government guidelines. Mothers today are widely expected to be able to crack an egg with one hand, quote Nabokov on prams *and* save a baby from choking — ideally, all at the same time.

The job thus demands a far broader skill set than ever before. But worry not: *How to Crack an Egg with One Hand: A Pocket Book for the New Mother* is here to help. Contained within these pages is everything a twenty-first-century new mother needs to know. Keep it in the back pocket of your maternity jeans or the front pocket of your nappy bag, by the loo or next to the kettle. It might just keep you sane.

BOOKS PUBLISHED IN BRITAIN PRIOR TO 1900 WITH THE WORD 'PREGNANCY' IN THE TITLE

Year	Title	Author
1554	A Copie of a Letter sent from the Counsell unto the Ryghte Reverende Father in God Edmonde Bysshoppe of London, Informing him of the Queen's supposed pregnancy . . .	Anonymous
1717	On the Signs of Pregnancy	Polycarp Gottlieb Schacher
1733	The Wanton Countess: or, Ten Thousand Pounds for a Pregnancy, a New Ballad Opera Founded on a True Secret History	Mortimer
1739	Aphorisms Relating to the Pregnancy, Delivery and Diseases of Women	François Mauriceau
1775	Practical Observations on the Child-bed Fever: also on the Nature and Treatment of Uterine Haemorrhages, Convulsions, and such other Acute Diseases as are most Fatal to Women during the State of Pregnancy . . .	John Leake
1777	Account of a Woman who had the Small Pox during Pregnancy, and Who Seemed to have Communicated the Same Disease to the Foetus	John Hunter
1777	A Letter to a Lady on the Mode of Conducting Herself during Pregnancy	S. Brown
1778	An Essay on the Evil Consequences Attending Injudicious Bleeding in Pregnancy	George Wallis

Year	Title	Author
1780	Lying In: Mr White's Address to the Community, respecting Conceal'd Pregnancy	Mr White
1785	An Essay on Uterine Haemorrhages depending on Pregnancy and Parturition	Thomas Denman
1786	The Singular Case of a Lady, who had the Small-Pox during Pregnancy; and who Communicated the Same Disease to the Foetus	Walter Lynn
1789	Advice to the Female Sex in General, especially Those in a State of Pregnancy and Lying In	John Grigg
1793	Practical Essays on the Management of Pregnancy and Labour	John Clarke
1797	The Pupil of Nature; or, Candid Advice to the Fair Sex on the Subject of Pregnancy, Childbirth	Martha Mears*
1797	Santa-Maria; or, the Mysterious Pregnancy. A romance.	Joseph Fox
1798	Cautions to Women, Respecting the State of Pregnancy	Seguin Henry Jackson
1799	The Anatomy of the Gravid Uterus, with Practical Inferences Relative to Pregnancy and Labour	John Burns
1806	Collects to be Said during the Pregnancy of the Vice-Queen August Amelia	Anonymous

* 'Take Nature's Path, and Mad Opinions Leave' is the fantastic quote, courtesy of Alexander Pope, with which this book opens. Martha Mears was a late-eighteenth-century gynaecologist and obstetrician whose main innovation in her book was to argue that 'A state of pregnancy has too generally been considered as a state of indisposition or disease: this is a fatal error and the source of almost all the evils to which women in childbearing are liable.'

Year	Title	Author
1815	*An Impartial Account of the Life and Writings of Joanna Southcott, Containing the Particulars Respecting her Miraculous Pregnancy**	Anonymous
1817	*An Address to British Females on the Moral Management of Pregnancy and Labour*	William Cooke and Charlotte Augusta, Consort of Leopold, Prince of Saxe-Coburg
1825	*An Attempt to Prove, on Rational Principles, that the Term of Human Pregnancy may be Considerably Extended Beyond Nine Calendar Months*	John Power
1826	*The Medical Evidence Relative to the Duration of Human Pregnancy*	Robert Lyall
1829	*An Essay on the Symptoms of Pregnancy, from the Earliest Stage to the Period of Quickening*	John Morley
1832	*A Practical Treatise on Uterine Haemorrhage in Connexion with Pregnancy and Parturition*	John Thomas Ingleby
1834	*The Signs, Disorders and Management of Pregnancy*	Douglas Fox
1837	*An Exposition on the Signs and Symptoms of Pregnancy*	William F. Montgomery
1837	*Hints to Mothers, for the Management of Health during the Period of Pregnancy*	Thomas Bull

---

* Born in Devon in 1750, Joanna Southcott worked as a domestic servant until her forties, at which point she decided she was more suited to being a prophetess, travelling the country and telling people how to save the world. At the age of sixty-four, she used her book *The Third Book of Wonders, Announcing the Coming of Shiloh; with a Call to the Hebrews* to inform the world she was pregnant with the Messiah. She died a few months later.

Year	Title	Author
1840	*Observations on the Diseases incident to Pregnancy and Childbed*	Fleetwood Churchill
1842	*The Young Wife's and Mother's Book. Advice to Mothers on the Management of their Offspring . . . Advice to Young Wives on the Management of Themselves during the Periods of Pregnancy and Lactation . . . , Second Edition, Considerably Enlarged and Improved*	Pye Henry Chavasse*
1849	*The Water-Cure in Pregnancy and Childbirth: Illustrated with Cases, showing the Remarkable Effects of Water in Mitigating the Pains . . . of the Parturient State*	Joel Shew
1852	*The Young Wife's Guide during Pregnancy and Childbirth*	Henry Davies
1852	*Corpulence or Excess of Fat during Pregnancy*	Thomas King Chambers
1855	*On the Statics of Pregnancy*	James Matthews Duncan
1860	*On the Signs and Diseases of Pregnancy*	Thomas Hawkes Tanner
1870	*Counsel to a Young Wife on the Rule of Conduct requisite during Pregnancy and Lying-in*	Henry Thomas Scott
1874	*On the Condition of the Mouth and Teeth during Pregnancy*	James Oakley Coles

---

* This book by a Birmingham obstetrician was the most popular infant-management manual of the century: it went into eighteen editions in its first fifty years alone. Chavasse answers all those questions that you too have been desperate to ask your health visitor, for example on page thirty-eight: 'If a child be suffering severely from wind, is there any objection to the addition of a very small quantity of gin or peppermint, to disperse it?' To which the answer is, boringly, 'It is a murderous practice to add gin or peppermint.' Oh well, just a thought.

Year	Title	Author
1875	Maternal Impressions: A Consideration of the Effect of Mental Disturbance during Pregnancy upon the Intellectual Development of the Child	Robert James Lee
1876	Extra-Uterine Pregnancy: Its Causes	John S. Parry
1877	The Signs and Concomitant Derangements of Pregnancy	William Morgan
1878	The Bearings of Chronic Disease of the Heart upon Pregnancy	Angus Macdonald
1882	The Diagnosis and Treatment of Diseases of Women, including the Diagnosis of Pregnancy	William Morse Graily Hewitt
1887	On the Ceremonies Observed among Hindus during Pregnancy and Parturition	Kānhobā Kīrtikara
1890	On Severe Vomiting during Pregnancy	William Morse Graily Hewitt
1893	A Handbook for Mothers: Being Simple Hints to Women on the Management of their Health during Pregnancy and Confinement	Jane Harriett Walker
1895	Ectopic Pregnancy	John Clarence Webster
1895	Pregnancy, Labor and the Puerpetal State	Egbert Henry Grandin
1899	Extra-Uterine Pregnancy	John William Taylor

YOGA

YOGA works wonders for pregnant women, specifically by soothingly engaging certain parts of the body that will soon know more exercise than ought to be legal. Regular indulgence in what originally developed out of ancient Indian asceticism culminates in a trouble-free pregnancy, natural birth and a speedy reintroduction of tight jeans – or so devotees claim. For those who need further persuasion, here are five additional reasons to brave a local yoga class of a rainy Tuesday evening.

- They are a reason to leave work early.
- They smell delicious, like a Catholic church.
- They are a way to meet other women in the same predic-ament, particularly if one's local NCT group is oversubscribed, or chaotically run.
- It is difficult to have huge amounts of fun in a pub these days, so yoga is a legitimate way of whiling away a few dull hours once night has fallen.
- It is an excuse to lie like a beached whale in a darkened room, where one cannot be roped into discussions about mortgages or the recession.

There is one serious risk involved, though: that is, the risk that one might be asked to chant. So beware. There are also some who are quite simply allergic to the prospect of a class of any sort, be it yoga 101, teach yourself brain surgery or how to survive on an international space station, because it is just too reminiscent of school. So here are a few yoga exercises to try at home instead. It is recommended, however, that you follow them under 'expert' supervision, as for maximum efficacy the exercises should be practised in conjunction with 'pranayamas' and other such business.

FIRST TRIMESTER

1. *Ardha Titali Asana (Half Butterfly)*

Right. Sit on the floor. Legs outstretched! Fold up right leg, and pop right foot as far up left thigh as you can. Place right hand atop folded right knee. Grasp toes of right foot with left hand. Whilst inhaling, slowly move right knee towards breasts. Exhaling, gently push knee down as if to touch the floor. Your body should not move. Any leg movement achieved should be through application of right arm. Repeat with the left limb. Creakily practise ten goes with each leg.

Benefits? Great for limbering up the hip joints, thereby encouraging a speedier delivery.

2. *Supta Udarakarshanasana (Sleeping Abdominal Stretch)*

Lie on back. Aaah, lovely. Fold up knees, planting soles of feet on floor. While exhaling, lower the legs to the right, attempting to meet the floor with the knees. Simultaneously, slide head round to the left, generating a healthy stretch along the length of the spine. Repeat on the opposite side by swinging legs over to the left, and bounce to the right.

Benefits? Alleviates spinal stiffness. Ameliorates digestion. Relieves constipation (though hopefully not there and then).

3. Marjariasana (Cat Stretch)

Crouch with buttocks perched on heels. Raise bottom and push weight on to knees. Pop hands flat on the ground. Breathe in whilst lifting the head and pushing the spine concave. Breathe out, dropping the bottom and stretching the spine to the ceiling. At the end of the out breath, suck in the stomach and tighten the buttocks. The head will now be nestled within the arms, looking out between legs. How appropriate! This constitutes one go. Repeat up to ten times, but do not overdo it.

Benefits? This stretch aims to increase flexibility of the spine. It is also meant to tone the reproductive system.

4. Kandharasana (Shoulder Pose)

Start horizontal on the floor. Bend the knees, keeping soles of feet squarely on the ground, heels nuzzling the buttocks. Grab hold of ankles. Lift buttocks and curve your poor aching back. Attempt to hoist the chest and stomach to maximum height, and do not cheat by shifting shoulders or toes. The body should be comfortably and stably supported by head, shoulders and feet. Hold like this as long as you can before crashing to earth. Crumbs.

Benefits? As well as sorting out the spine, this stretch is thought to be good for the digestion, by stretching out (eek!) the colon and other organs. Surprisingly, given its rakish angle, it is particularly advised for ladies with a tendency to miscarry. Under professional supervision, this is also the one that is sometimes employed to turn a breech baby.

SECOND TRIMESTER

1. *Matsya Kridasana (Flapping Fish. Nice.)*

Plonk yourself sort of on front, with bump out of the way and fingers intertwined underneath the head. Fold right leg out to the side, bringing right knee up to chat to the ribs – if you can remember what they are. Keep the left leg straight. Prop right elbow atop right knee (or, if this is vastly uncomfortable, rest it on the ground) and lay the left side of head atop right arm. Aaah. Relax. When you have had enough of this and are beginning to think of supper, change sides.

Benefits? This position is said to ease pressure on the nerves in the pins. During the latter months of pregnancy, lying on your back is really uncomfortable, as – alarmingly – some major veins get squashed. This pose is thus recommended for sleeping. Special pillows can be purchased to anchor yourself down accordingly.

2. *Vajrasana (Thunderbolt)*

Kneeling, slide the big toes together and prise apart the heels. Release the buttocks on to the instep, heels pressed to the hips. Pop hands on lap, palms facing downwards. Keep back and head straight, but not stiffly so.

Benefits? An alternative to antacids for relieving stomach ailments (which are a common curse of pregnancy). It is also believed to fortify the pelvic muscles, thereby preparing you for the increasingly impending birth. Well, in some ways, perhaps.

3. *Meru Akarshanasana (Spinal Bending Pose. Crikey.)*

Recline on left side of body, right leg atop left. Support head atop left arm. Pop right arm on to right thigh. Raise right leg as high as you dare, moving the right hand up to the foot and seizing the big toe. Repeat with other leg.

Benefits? Good luck. But if you *can* manage this, it is meant to loosen up the hamstrings and tummy muscles.

THIRD TRIMESTER

1. Poorna Titali Asana (Full Butterfly)

As with Half Butterfly, plant yourself on your bottom, legs stretched out in front. Fold the knees and draw together the soles of your feet, bringing in the heels as tightly towards the body as your increasing bulk allows. Attempt to completely release any inside thigh tension. Grasp feet with both hands. Carefully bounce your knees about, pushing them down using the elbows. Gently, gently, remembering one's condition. Repeat for up to thirty goes. Aaaand . . . relax!

Benefits? Relieves general leg exhaustion, as well as tightness of the inside thigh. Can it do anything about the varicose veins, though?

2. Shoulder Rotation (shame about the inauthentic name)

Elevate the arms, fingertip atop shoulders. Gently rotate the arms simultaneously in ever-increasing circles. Pull the elbows as far as you dare, and attempt to encourage them to meet in front. Try five times each way. Breathe in as the chest expands, with the elbows moving to the rear. Breathe out as your elbows creak towards each other out front.

Benefits? Practising this stretch throughout pregnancy and after the birth stimulates optimal functioning of your soon-to-be-taxed mammary glands.

3. Ankle Crank (terribly onomatopoeic, one imagines)

Sitting on the floor, bring your right leg atop the left, so that the foot flaps over the left knee. Clasp your right toes with the left hand. Support your right ankle with right hand. Crack I mean crank I mean ouch! the flopping ankle all about in a generous manner, stretching as far as it will go without snapping off. Perform ten rounds, first to the left, and then to the right. Repeat with the left ankle.

Benefits? Helps with swelling, cramps and rubbish circulation, and is (apparently) also particularly helpful in relieving post-epidural numbness of the pins.

MATERNITY LEAVE BENEFITS

(listed alphabetically, from A to M only)

Country	Length of maternity leave	Percentage of wages paid in covered period	Provider of medical benefit
Afghanistan	90 days	100 per cent	Employer
Albania	365 calendar days	80 per cent prior to birth and for 150 days, and 50 per cent for the rest of the leave period	Social insurance system
Algeria	14 weeks	100 per cent	Social security
America, the United States of	12 weeks	There is no national programme, although cash benefits are sometimes provided at the state level. It is one of only four countries (the others are Swaziland, Liberia and Papua New Guinea) that does not provide or require employers to provide some form of maternity leave.	—
Andorra	16 weeks	100 per cent	Social insurance system
Angola	3 months	100 per cent	Social security (if necessary, the employer adds up to the full wage)
Antigua and Barbuda	13 weeks	60 per cent	Social insurance system and supplemented by employer
Argentina	90 days	100 per cent	Family allowance funds (financed through state and employer contributions)

Country	Length of maternity leave	Percentage of wages paid in covered period	Provider of medical benefit
Armenia	140 days	100 per cent	Social insurance
Australia	52 weeks	A lump sum payment is paid for each child. Otherwise unpaid. Improved provisions are being introduced in 2011, however.	Universal and social assistance systems
Austria	16 weeks	100 per cent	Statutory health insurance, family burden equalization fund or employer
Azerbaijan	126 calendar days	100 per cent	Social insurance
Bahamas	13 weeks	100 per cent	The National Insurance Board (two-thirds) and the employer (one-third)
Bahrain	45 days	100 per cent	Employer
Bangladesh	12 weeks	100 per cent	Employer
Barbados	12 weeks	100 per cent	National insurance system
Belarus	126 days	100 per cent	State social insurance
Belgium	15 weeks	82 per cent for the first 30 days and 75 per cent for the remaining period (up to a ceiling)	Social security
Belize	12 weeks	80 per cent	Social security or employer (for women who are not entitled to receive benefits from social security)

Country	Length of maternity leave	Percentage of wages paid in covered period	Provider of medical benefit
Benin	14 weeks	100 per cent	50 per cent social security, 50 per cent employer
Bermuda	12 weeks	100 per cent. (No statutory benefits are provided. However, the 2000 Employment Act provides for 8 weeks paid and 4 weeks unpaid maternity leave to employees who have worked for the same employer for at least a year; 8 weeks unpaid maternity leave for employees with less than a year.)	Employer
Bolivia	60 days (90 days for domestic workers)	95 per cent (benefit paid for up to 45 days before and 45 days after the expected date of child-birth)	Social insurance
Bosnia and Herzegovina	1 year	100 per cent	Not available
Botswana	12 weeks	25 per cent	Employer
Brazil	120 days	100 per cent	Social insurance
British Virgin Islands	13 weeks	67 per cent	Social insurance
Bulgaria	135 days	90 per cent	Public social insurance (the General Sickness and Maternity Fund)

Country	Length of maternity leave	Percentage of wages paid in covered period	Provider of medical benefit
Burkina Faso	14 weeks	100 per cent	Social security and employer
Burundi	12 weeks	50 per cent	Employer
Cambodia	90 days	50 per cent	Employer
Cameroon	14 weeks	100 per cent	The National Social Insurance Fund
Canada	17–18 weeks (duration depends on the province)	55 per cent (up to a ceiling)	Federal and State Employment Insurance
Cape Verde	45 days	90 per cent	Social insurance
Central African Republic	14 weeks	50 per cent	Social security
Chad	14 weeks	50 per cent	Social insurance
Channel Islands, Guernsey	18 weeks	Flat rate	Social insurance and social assistance
Channel Islands, Jersey	18 weeks	Flat rate	Social insurance
Chile	18 weeks	100 per cent	Social security
China	90 days	100 per cent	Employer
Colombia	12 weeks	100 per cent	Social security
Comoros	14 weeks	100 per cent	Employer

Country	Length of maternity leave	Percentage of wages paid in covered period	Provider of medical benefit
Congo	15 weeks	100 per cent	50 per cent social security, 50 per cent employer
Costa Rica	4 months	100 per cent	50 per cent social security, 50 per cent employer
Côte d'Ivoire	14 weeks	100 per cent	The National Social Insurance Fund
Croatia	1+ year (45 days before delivery and 1 year after)	100 per cent until the child reaches the age of six months, and then at a level determined by the Act on the Execution of the State Budget for the remaining period	Health Insurance Fund (until the child reaches the age of 6 months); the rest is paid from the State Budget
Cuba	18 weeks	100 per cent	Social security
Cyprus	16 weeks	75 per cent	Social security
Czech Republic	28 weeks	69 per cent	Social security
Democratic Republic of the Congo	14 weeks	67 per cent	Employer
Denmark	52 weeks	100 per cent (up to a ceiling)	Municipality and employer
Djibouti	14 weeks	50 per cent (100 per cent for public servants)	Employer
Dominica	12 weeks	60 per cent	Social security and employer

Country	Length of maternity leave	Percentage of wages paid in covered period	Provider of medical benefit
Dominican Republic	12 weeks	100 per cent	50 per cent social security, 50 per cent employer
Ecuador	8 weeks	100 per cent	75 per cent social security, 25 per cent employer
Egypt	90 days	100 per cent	Social security and employer
El Salvador	12 weeks	75 per cent	Social security for insured workers, otherwise employer must pay
Equatorial Guinea	12 weeks	75 per cent	Social security
Eritrea	60 days	Paid amount not specified	Employer
Estonia	140 calendar days	100 per cent	Health Insurance Fund
Ethiopia	90 days	100 per cent	Employer for up to 45 days
Fiji	84 days	Flat rate	Employer
Finland	105 working days	70 per cent	Social insurance system
France	16 weeks	100 per cent (up to a ceiling)	Social security
Gabon	14 weeks	50 per cent	Social insurance system
Gambia	12 weeks	100 per cent	Employer

Country	Length of maternity leave	Percentage of wages paid in covered period	Provider of medical benefit
Germany	14 weeks	100 per cent	Statutory health insurance scheme, state, employer
Ghana	12 weeks	No statutory benefits are provided	–
Great Britain and Northern Ireland	52 weeks (consisting of 26 weeks of Ordinary Maternity Leave and 26 weeks of Additional Maternity Leave)	90 per cent (statutory maternity leave is paid for a continuous period of up to 39 weeks at a rate of 90 per cent for the first 6 weeks, then a flat rate for the remaining weeks)	Employer (92 per cent refunded by public funds)
Greece	119 days	100 per cent	Social security/employer
Grenada	3 months	100 per cent for 2 months and 60 per cent for the final month	60 per cent for 12 weeks by social security, 40 per cent for 2 months by employer
Guatemala	84 days	100 per cent	Two-thirds social security, one-third employer
Guinea	14 weeks	100 per cent	50 per cent social security, 50 per cent employer
Guinea-Bissau	60 days	100 per cent	Employer (if a woman affiliated to a social security scheme receives a subsidy, the employer pays the difference between the subsidy and the salary)

Country	Length of maternity leave	Percentage of wages paid in covered period	Provider of medical benefit
Guyana	13 weeks	70 per cent	Social security
Haiti	12 weeks	100 per cent for 6 weeks, 0 per cent thereafter	Employer
Honduras	10 weeks	100 per cent	Two-thirds social security, one-third employer
Hong Kong	10 weeks	80 per cent	Employer
Hungary	24 weeks	70 per cent	Social insurance system
Iceland	3 months	80 per cent	Social security
India	12 weeks	100 per cent	Social security or employer (for non-covered women)
Indonesia	3 months	100 per cent	Employer
Iran	90 days	67 per cent	Social security
Iraq	62 days	100 per cent	Social security
Ireland	18 weeks	70 per cent	Social Insurance Fund
Isle of Man	26 weeks	90 per cent (up to a ceiling)	Social insurance and social assistance system
Israel	12 weeks	100 per cent (up to a ceiling)	Social security
Italy	5 months	80 per cent	Social security
Jamaica	12 weeks	100 per cent for 8 weeks, 0 per cent thereafter	Employer

Country	Length of maternity leave	Percentage of wages paid in covered period	Provider of medical benefit
Japan	14 weeks	60 per cent	Health insurance scheme (if managed by employer) or Social Insurance Agency (if managed by the government)
Jordan	10 weeks	100 per cent	Employer
Kazakhstan	126 calendar days	100 per cent	Employer
Kenya	2 months	100 per cent	Employer
Kiribati	12 weeks	25 per cent	Employer
Kuwait	70 days	100 per cent	Employer
Kyrgyzstan	126 calendar days	100 per cent	Social security
Lao People's Democratic Republic	90 days	100 per cent. (Coverage is limited to employees in private-sector and state-owned enterprises with 10 or more employees, and pensioners. Coverage is available only in certain regions of the country.)	Social security or employer
Latvia	112 calendar days	100 per cent	State Social Insurance
Lebanon	7 weeks	100 per cent	Employer
Lesotho	12 weeks	No legal obligation for paid maternity leave but some employment contracts have provision	Employer

Country	Length of maternity leave	Percentage of wages paid in covered period	Provider of medical benefit
Libyan Arab Jamahiriya	50 days	50 per cent (100 per cent for self-employed women)	Employer (social security for self-employed women)
Liechtenstein	20 weeks	80 per cent	Social insurance
Lithuania	126 calendar days	100 per cent	State Social Insurance Fund
Luxembourg	16 weeks	100 per cent	Social insurance
Madagascar	14 weeks	100 per cent	50 per cent social insurance, 50 per cent employer
Malawi	8 weeks (every 3 years)	100 per cent	Employer
Malaysia	60 days	100 per cent	Employer
Mali	14 weeks	100 per cent	Social security
Malta	14 weeks	100 per cent for 13 weeks, 0 per cent thereafter	Employer
Mauritania	14 weeks	100 per cent	Social Security Fund
Mauritius	12 weeks	100 per cent	Employer
Mexico	12 weeks	100 per cent	Social security
Monaco	16 weeks	90 per cent (up to a ceiling)	Social insurance
Mongolia	120 days	70 per cent	Social Insurance Fund
Morocco	14 weeks	100 per cent	Social security
Mozambique	60 days	100 per cent	Employer
Myanmar	12 weeks	67 per cent	Social insurance

Source: United Nations Department of Economic and Social Affairs

THE ORIGINS OF SOME MAJOR HUMAN CHARACTERISTICS

Language	*100,000 years ago*
Brain size	*500,000 years ago*
Carnivorous	*2,500,000 years ago*
Small canines	*3,200,000 years ago*
Bipedalism (i.e. the ability to walk on two legs, rather than four)	*5,000,000 years ago*
Tricolour vision	*23,000,000 years ago*
Dental pattern	*35 million years ago*
Three ear ossicles (tiny bones inside the ear that give humans very acute hearing)	*130 million years ago*
Hair	*150 million years ago*
Five fingers and five toes	*340 million years ago*
Two arms and two legs	*385 million years ago*
Jaws	*460 million years ago*
Three semicircular canals (interconnected tubes inside the ear that give humans excellent balance)	*470 million years ago*
Backbone	*520 million years ago*
Two eyes	*550 million years ago*

MOST POPULAR GIRLS' NAMES IN ENGLAND AND WALES OVER THE PAST 300 YEARS;

	1700	1800	1850	1875	1900	1925	1935
1	Mary	Mary	Mary	Mary	Florence	Joan	Shirley
2	Elizabeth	Ann	Elizabeth	Elizabeth	Mary	Mary	Margaret
3	Ann	Elizabeth	Sarah	Sarah	Alice	Joyce	Jean
4	Sarah	Sarah	Ann	Annie	Annie	Margaret	Joan
5	Jane	Jane	Eliza	Alice	Elsie	Dorothy	Patricia
6	Margaret	Hannah	Jane	Florence	Edith	Doris	Mary
7	Susan	Susan	Emma	Emily	Elizabeth	Kathleen	Sheila
8	Martha	Martha	Hannah	Edith	Doris	Irene	Doreen
9	Hannah	Margaret	Ellen	Ellen	Dorothy	Betty	Sylvia
10	Catherine	Charlotte	Martha	Ada*	Ethel	Eileen	Barbara
11	Alice	Harriet	Emily	Margaret	Gladys	Doreen	Audrey
12	Frances	Betty	Harriet	Ann	Lilian	Lilian	Maureen
13	Eleanor	Maria	Alice	Emma	Hilda	Vera	Brenda
14	Dorothy	Catherine	Margaret	Jane	Margaret	Jean	Dorothy
15	Rebecca	Frances	Maria	Eliza	Winifred	Marjorie	June
16	Isabel	Mary-Ann	Louisa	Louisa	Lily	Barbara	Pamela
17	Grace	Nancy	Fanny	Clara	Ellen	Edna	Joyce
18	Joan	Rebecca	Caroline	Martha	Ada	Gladys	Beryl
19	Rachel	Alice	Charlotte	Harriet	Emily	Audrey	Eileen
20	Agnes	Ellen	Susannah	Hannah	Violet	Elsie	Ann

---

* History's most famous Ada is Ada, Countess of Lovelace (1815–52), who is widely considered the world's first computer programmer. Her reputation is founded upon a series of notes she wrote about a new kind of calculating machine invented by Charles Babbage known as an Analytical Engine. Her father was the poet Lord Byron, and she named one of her children Byron after him; the other two were named Ralph and Anne.

OR, WHATEVER HAPPENED TO ALL THE MARYS?

	1950	1965	1975	1985	1993	2008
1	Susan	Trac(e)y*	Claire	Sarah	Rebecca	Olivia
2	Linda	Deborah	Sarah	Claire	Charlotte	Ruby
3	Christine	Julie	Nicola	Emma	Laura	Emily
4	Margaret	Karen	Emma	Laura	Amy	Grace
5	Carol	Susan	Joanne	Rebecca	Emma	Jessica
6	Jennifer	Alison	Helen	Gemma	Jessica	Chloe
7	Janet	Jacqueline	Rachel	Rachel	Lauren	Sophie
8	Patricia	Helen	Lisa	Kelly	Sarah	Lily
9	Barbara	Amanda	Rebecca	Victoria	Rachel	Amelia
10	Ann	Sharon	Karen	Katherine	Catherine	Evie
11	Sandra	Sarah	Michelle	Katie	Hannah	Mia
12	Pamela	Joanne	Victoria	Nicola	Katie	Ella
13	Pauline	Jane	Catherine	Jennifer	Emily	Charlotte
14	Jean	Catherine	Amanda	Natalie	Sophie	Lucy
15	Jacqueline	Angela	Trac(e)y	Hayley	Victoria	Megan
16	Kathleen	Linda	Samantha	Michelle	Stacey	Ellie
17	Sheila	Carol	Kelly	Amy	Natalie	Isabelle
18	Valerie	Diane	Deborah	Lisa	Jade	Isabella
19	Maureen	Wendy†	Julie	Lindsay	Stephanie	Hannah
20	Gillian	Beverley	Louise	Samantha	Lucy	Katie

---

* Well-known Trac(e)ys include comedian Tracey Ullman, the mercifully-never-dull artist Tracy Emin and 'Tracey the barmaid', the longest-serving (no pun intended) female character in *EastEnders*, who has been a fixture behind the bar since the programme's very first episode in 1985.

† Wendy was an extremely rare name, only ever used as a diminutive of Gwendolyn, until it was popularized by J.M. Barrie in his 1911 novel *Peter Pan*, which opens with the following lines: 'All children, except one, grow up. They soon know that they will grow up, and the way Wendy knew was this. One day when she was two years old she was playing in a garden, and she plucked another flower and ran with it to her mother. I suppose she must have looked rather delightful, for Mrs Darling put her hand to her heart and cried, "Oh, why can't you remain like this for ever!" This was all that passed between them on the subject, but henceforth Wendy knew that she must grow up. You always know after you are two. Two is the beginning of the end.'

MOST POPULAR BOYS' NAMES IN ENGLAND AND WALES OVER THE PAST 300 YEARS;

	1700	1800	1850	1875	1900	1925	1935
1	John*	William	William	William	William	John	John
2	William	John	John	John	John	William	Brian
3	Thomas	Thomas	George	George	George	George	Peter
4	Richard	James	Thomas	Thomas	Thomas	James	Ronald
5	James	George	James	James	Charles	Ronald	Michael
6	Robert	Joseph	Henry	Henry	Frederick	Robert	Alan
7	Joseph	Richard	Charles	Charles	Arthur	Kenneth	William
8	Edward	Henry	Joseph	Frederick	James	Frederick	David
9	Henry	Robert	Robert	Arthur	Albert	Thomas	Kenneth
10	George	Charles	Samuel	Joseph	Ernest	Albert	George
11	Samuel	Samuel	Edward	Albert†	Robert	Eric	Derek
12	Francis	Edward	Frederick	Alfred	Henry	Edward	James
13	Charles	Benjamin	Alfred	Walter	Alfred	Arthur	Robert
14	Daniel	Isaac	Richard	Harry	Sidney	Charles	Donald
15	Benjamin	Peter	Walter	Edward	Joseph	Leslie	Colin
16	Edmund	Daniel	Arthur	Robert	Harold	Sidney	Raymond
17	Matthew	David	Benjamin	Ernest	Harry	Frank	Roy
18	Peter	Francis	David	Herbert	Frank	Peter	Thomas
19	Nicholas	Stephen	Edwin	Sidney§	Walter	Dennis	Anthony
20	Isaac	Jonathan	Albert	Samuel	Herbert	Joseph	Dennis

---

*   John in Lithuanian is Jonas; in Latvian it is Jānis.

†   Every time Queen Victoria presented Prince Albert with a new baby, he would give her a commemorative locket containing a few strands of the baby's hair and engraved with the date. The two of them had a total of nine children together, so the Queen's jewellery box must have been quite close to overflowing by the time Albert's death in 1861 at the age of just forty-two brought the marriage to a tragically abrupt end.

§   Well-known Sidneys include Sidney Poitier (yay!), Sid Vicious (boo!) and Sidney Pullen, who, in 1916–17, became the only foreigner (he was born in South-ampton) ever to play for the Brazilian national football team.

OR, WHATEVER HAPPENED TO ALL THE JOHNS?

	1950	1965	1975	1985	1993	2008
1	David	Paul	Stephen	Christopher	Daniel	Jack
2	John	David	Mark	Matthew	Matthew	Oliver
3	Peter	Andrew	Paul	David	James	Thomas
4	Michael	Stephen	Andrew	James	Christopher	Harry
5	Alan	Mark	David	Daniel	Thomas	Joshua
6	Robert	Michael	Richard	Andrew	Joshua	Alfie
7	Stephen	Ian	Matthew	Steven	Adam	Charlie
8	Paul	Gary	Daniel	Michael	Michael	Daniel
9	Brian	Robert	Christopher	Mark	Luke	James
10	Graham	Richard	Darren	Paul	Andrew	William
11	Philip	Peter	Michael	Richard	Benjamin	Samuel
12	Anthony	John	James	Adam	Samuel	George
13	Colin	Anthony	Robert	Robert	Stephen	Joseph
14	Christopher	Christopher	Simon	Lee	Robert	Lewis
15	Geoffrey	Darren	Jason	Craig	Jamie	Ethan
16	William	Kevin	Stuart	Benjamin	Aaron	Mohammed
17	James	Martin	Neil	Thomas	Jonathan	Dylan
18	Keith	Simon	Lee	Peter	Alexander	Benjamin
19	Terence	Philip	Jonathan	Anthony	Joseph	Alexander
20	Barry	Graham	Ian	Shaun	Ryan	Jacob

BABYMOON

CONSIDERING a babymoon? Oh do, do. Here are *Condé Nast Traveler*'s Top Hotels and Resorts in the World.

1. Four Seasons Tented Camp Golden Triangle, Chiang Rai, Thailand
2. Peninsula House, Dominican Republic
3. Blanket Bay, South Island, New Zealand
4. La Scalinatella, Capri, Italy
=. King Pacific Lodge, British Columbia, Canada
6. 21c Museum Hotel, Louisville, Kentucky, USA
=. La Colombe d'Or, St-Paul de Vence, France
=. Oberoi Udaivilas, Rajasthan, India
=. Oberoi Vanyavilas, Rajasthan, India
10. Mombo and Little Mombo Camps, Botswana
11. Il San Pietro di Positano, Positano, Italy
12. Ritz-Carlton, Tokyo, Japan
13. The Peninsula, Hong Kong, People's Republic of China
=. Four Seasons Resort Bali at Sayan, Bali, Indonesia
15. One&Only Palmilla, Los Cabos, Baja, California, USA
16. Hotel Taschenbergpalais Kempinski Dresden, Germany
=. The Saxon, Johannesburg, South Africa
18. Sandibe Safari Lodge, Botswana
19. Grand Hotel a Villa Feltrinelli, Lake Garda, Italy
=. Il Pellicano, Porto Ercole, Tuscany, Italy
21. Oberoi Amarvilas, Agra, India
=. The Peninsula, Chicago, USA
=. Safari Lodges at Phinda Private Game Reserve, South Africa

24. Four Seasons Resort Maui at Wailea, Maui, USA
25. Four Seasons Hotel Gresham Palace Budapest, Budapest, Hungary
 =. Mandarin Oriental, Bangkok, Thailand
27. Singita Sabi Sand, South Africa
28. Four Seasons Hotel George V, Paris, France
29. Grande Roche Hotel, Paarl, South Africa
30. Grand-Hôtel du Cap-Ferrat, Côte d'Azur, France
 =. The Peninsula, Bangkok, Thailand
 =. Jao Camp, Botswana
 =. Wildflower Hall, Shimla, India
34. Four Seasons Resort, Langkawi, Malaysia
35. Oberoi Rajvilas, Rajasthan, India
36. Chewton Glen, Hampshire, England
 =. Pudong Shangri-La, Shanghai, People's Republic of China
 =. Burj Al Arab, Dubai
 =. Kenwood Inn and Spa, Sonoma, California, USA
40. Four Seasons Resort Istanbul at Sultanahmet, Istanbul, Turkey
41. The Tides, Riviera Maya, Mexico
42. Le Sirenuse, Positano, Italy
 =. Ritz-Carlton, Berlin, Germany
 =. Ritz-Carlton Beijing, Financial Street, Beijing, People's Republic of China
45. Four Seasons Hotel Firenze, Florence, Italy
 =. Hôtel Ritz Paris, Paris, France
 =. Mandarin Oriental, Boston, USA
 =. Savuti Camp, Botswana
49. Baur au Lac, Zurich, Switzerland
 =. Four Seasons Resort, Sharm El Sheikh, Egypt

DNA: AN EXPLANATION

DNA is what makes your baby your baby: it determines hair colour, eye colour, liking for chips and disliking for fish, risk of cancer, whether or not he or she is prone to depression, and everything else in between.

DNA, which is an abbreviation for deoxyribonucleic acid, is a molecule that contains all the instructions that are passed from adults to babies during the reproductive process to make them what they are, and to develop and direct them.

Most of the DNA is found inside the cell's nucleus (apart from a little bit of DNA that is found in the cell's mitochondria). Rather than being tightly packed, however, DNA has the ability to unwind when the cell divides, in order to allow itself to be copied to new cells. At this stage, it is in the shape of a double helix.

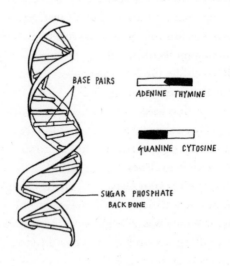

BASE PAIRS

ADENINE THYMINE

GUANINE CYTOSINE

SUGAR PHOSPHATE
BACK BONE

As well as a double helix, its physical appearance can be described as a little like a twisted ladder. Each rung of the ladder contains chemical building blocks, of which there are four types: adenine, cytosine, guanine and thymine, abbreviated with the letters A, C, G and T respectively. The order in which these letters are stacked in the ladder dictates how a person is built — for example, whether he or she will have blue eyes or brown eyes.

These letters are strung together in three-letter 'words', which in turn are strung in sentences, and each sentence of DNA constitutes a gene. A gene gives the cell instructions about how to make a specific protein, and proteins build up to create your baby.

Each gene coiled together in a form that can be duplicated is called a chromosome. A human has 46 bundles of DNA called chromosomes: 23 from the mother and 23 from the father. Taken together, the complete set of the DNA found in the cell's nucleus is called the genome. Each genome contains about 20,500 genes. The genomes of any two humans are 99 per cent the same; it is just the remaining 1 per cent that makes the difference.

The information in a gene's DNA is copied by means of an enzyme on to a molecule known as messenger ribonucleic acid RNA (mRNA). The mRNA is then decoded by another sort of molecule called a ribosome, which in turn links small molecules called amino acids together in a particular way to create a specific protein, whether a protein to make the heart or the skin, or to carry signals from brain to limb, or to control a chemical reaction to illness.

In 2003, the Human Genome Project completed the truly extraordinary scientific feat of mapping the entire human genetic map. Which was jolly clever of them indeed. Next time you are noodling around on your computer, you could do worse than visiting the project's website: www.genome.gov.

ICE CREAM

'WHAT a pity it isn't illegal,' mused Voltaire on the subject of ice cream. And while French philosophers tend not to have much in common with pregnant women, when it comes to ice cream they are united as one in their love of the stuff. This is not just because pregnant women need the calories: it is also because, for the first time ever, it suddenly becomes socially acceptable to demand one's partner traipses off to the supermarket at any time of day or night, just as long as one dresses it up in the guise of a 'craving'. So with this in mind, here is a list of every flavour (excluding limited editions) that Häagen-Dazs makes.

Almond Hazelnut Swirl
Baileys® Irish cream
Banana Split
Banoffee
Belgian Chocolate
Black Raspberry Chip
Black Walnut
Butter Pecan
Caramel Cone
Cherry Vanilla
Chocolate
Chocolate Chip
Chocolate Chip Cookie
   Dough
Chocolate Peanut Butter
Cinnamon Dulce de Leche

Coconut Macaroon
Coffee
Cookies and Cream
Crème Brûlée
Dulce de Leche
English Toffee
Honey Vanilla
Lychee
Macadamia Nut Brittle
Mango
Mayan Chocolate
Mint Chip
Mocha Almond Fudge
Mocha Chip
Pannacotta
Peaches and Cream

Pineapple Coconut
Pistachio
Pralines and Cream
Rocky Road
Rum Raisin
Sticky Toffee Pudding
(previously 2006 limited-
edition flavour)
Strawberry
Strawberry Cheesecake
Triple Chocolate
Vanilla
Vanilla Bean
Vanilla Chocolate Chip

Vanilla Fudge Brownie (also
known as Vanilla Caramel
Brownie)
Vanilla Honey Bee
Vanilla Swiss Almond
Waffle Cone
White Chocolate Raspberry
Truffle
Green Tea (China, Japan,
South Korea, USA, Hong
Kong, Taiwan, Malaysia,
Thailand and Singapore
only)
Azuki (Japan only)

Alternatively, make your own ice cream, starting with an old classic: vanilla.

250ml milk
1 vanilla pod
4 egg yolks
100g sugar
250ml double cream

Pour the milk into a saucepan and heat it slowly until it is nearly but not actually boiling. Cut the vanilla pod in half lengthways, scrape out the seeds into the milk, and then add the pod too. Take the milk off the heat and leave it to cool for at least 20 minutes.

In a bowl, beat together the egg yolks and sugar until the mixture is thick, lighter in colour and of a ribbon consistency (meaning that when you lift the whisk up, the mixture falls gently in ribbons). It is much easier to do this with an electric whisk if you have one, but with a hand whisk you will achieve the same result eventually.

Having removed the vanilla pod from the milk, pour the egg mixture into it and return to a low heat, stirring gently. Do not let the milk bubble or come to the boil. It should cook slowly until it thickens. The test is that when you dip a spoon into it, the mixture should form a coating over the back of the spoon. Essentially what you have before you is custard.

Assuming you are able to restrain yourself at this point from diving in and scoffing all the custard as is, leave it to cool completely. Then stir in the cream and pour the mixture into a wide, shallow dish. Put this in the freezer for about an hour, or until it is starting to freeze around the edges but not in the middle. Then take it out of the freezer and beat the mixture well to make a smooth consistency again and break up the ice crystals. Return to the freezer for another hour, mix again, and return to the freezer for another hour. Finally, about half an hour before you want to eat it, remove the ice cream from the freezer and put it in the fridge to soften a little.

Voltaire would be proud.

TOP FIVE SLANG WORDS FOR 'PREGNANT'

Knocked up	Bun in the oven
Up the duff	In the pudding club
Up the spout	

FISH

WHAT to eat and drink when pregnant is a subject of considerable controversy. *Plus ça change*: according to Pliny in his *Natural History* (c.AD 77–9), 'women who eat food that is too salty give birth to children without nails'. In France they don't eat lettuce, in Japan they do eat sushi, and so it goes on. Do approach such restrictions with a little bit of scepticism: the reason that almost all of them are there is merely to ensure you do not contract listeriosis, an extremely rare form of food poisoning resulting from the ingestion of the listeria bacteria, of which there have been only two cases in Britain in the last twenty years. The one dietary recommendation for pregnant women that (almost) everyone agrees upon, however, is the benefit of eating a lot of fish, due to their high quota of all-important Omega-3s. So here is a guide to what sort of fish to choose, according to which are from well-managed, under-fished sustainable stocks, which are from badly managed, over-fished, unsustainable stocks and which fall somewhere in between, eco-wise.

Species	Eat these often	Eat these occasionally	Never eat these
Abalone	• farmed		
Alaska or walleye pollock	• Marine Stewardship Council certified		
Anchovy		• Portuguese coast	• Bay of Biscay
Bib or pouting	•		

Species	Eat these often	Eat these occasionally	Never eat these
Black bream, porgy or seabream	•		
Clam	• American hardshell and manila, hand-gathered farmed sources	• dredge caught	
Cockle	• Marine Stewardship Council certified or hand gathered	• dredge caught	
Cod, Atlantic		• wild caught from north-east Arctic, Iceland, west English Channel, Bristol Channel and south-east Ireland	• wild caught from all other areas
Cod, Pacific	• Marine Stewardship Council certified		
Coley or saithe	• Marine Stewardship Council certified	• from Iceland or Faroes	
Crab	• edible/brown, pot caught from south Devon, or spider, pot caught	• edible/brown, pot caught	
Dab	•		
Dublin Bay prawn, scampi or langoustine	• Marine Stewardship Council certified	• west Scotland, North Sea, Skaggerak and Kattegat	• from Spain or Portugal
Flounder	•		
Gurnard	• grey and red	• yellow or tub	

Species	Eat these often	Eat these occasionally	Never eat these
Haddock		• north-east Arctic and North Sea, Skaggerak and Kattegat	• from Faroes and west Scotland
Hake		• Cape, Marine Stewardship Council certified	• European, southern stock
Halibut		• Pacific, Marine Stewardship Council certified	• Atlantic, wild caught
Halibut, Greenland		• from north-east Arctic	• from north-west Atlantic and Greenland, Iceland, west Scotland and Azores
Herring or sild	• from Norwegian stocks	• Marine Stewardship Council certified	• South Clyde, west Ireland and Great Sole fisheries
Ling		• handline caught from Faroes	• all other stocks
Lobster	• Western Australian rock, Marine Stewardship Council certified	• European	• from Canadian and south New England stocks
Mackerel		• Marine Stewardship Council certified	
Monkfish or anglerfish		• from south-west UK and north-east USA	• from north/ north-west Spain and Portugal
Mussel	• rope grown or hand gathered		
Oyster	• farmed native and Pacific		

Species	Eat these often	Eat these occasionally	Never eat these
Plaice		• otter trawled from Irish Sea, or gill/seine net from North Sea	• west English Channel, Celtic Sea, south-west Ireland and west Ireland
Pollack or lythe	•		
Prawn	• coldwater, from north-east Arctic	• tiger organically farmed, coldwater from north Pacific	• tiger, farmed and wild caught
Ray		• Cuckoo and spotted from North Sea, Skaggerak, east English Channel and Celtic Sea; starry from North Sea, Skaggerak and east English Channel	• smalleyed and thornback from Bay of Biscay; all blonde, sandy, shagreen and undulate
Red mullet	• from north-east Atlantic	• from Mediterranean	
Salmon	• Pacific or organically farmed	• Atlantic, farmed	• Atlantic, wild caught
Sardine or pilchard	• from Cornwall	• from Spain and Portugal	
Seabass	• line caught	• farmed	• pelagic trawled
Skate			•
Snapper	• red, from Western Australia trap fishery; Malabar blood from Western Australia	• vermilion and lane, silk and yellowtail	• cubera, mutton and northern red
Sole	• common or Dover, Marine Stewardship Council certified; lemon, otter trawl caught	• common or Dover, from east English Channel and south-west Ireland	• common or Dover from North Sea and Irish Sea

Species	Eat these often	Eat these occasionally	Never eat these
Squid	• jig caught	• trawl caught	
Swordfish			• Indian Ocean, Mediterranean and central and west Pacific
Tilapia	• farmed		
Trout	• brown or sea and rainbow, organically farmed	• brown or sea and rainbow, farmed	• brown or sea, wild caught from Baltic
Tuna, albacore	• Marine Stewardship Council certified	• from north Pacific or pole and line caught from north Atlantic	• longline and pelagic trawled from Mediterranean and north and south Atlantic
Tuna, bigeye		• handline and pole and line caught from central and west Pacific	• all other stocks
Tuna, blue fin			•
Tuna, skipjack	• pole and line from west/central Pacific or Maldives	• from Indian Ocean	• purse seine from west Atlantic
Tuna, yellowfin		•	
Turbot		• farmed	• wild caught

Source: Marine Conservation Society

'THE TINY MADMAN IN HIS PADDED CELL' (VLADIMIR NABOKOV); OR, THE DEVELOPMENT OF YOUR UNBORN BABY

1 week	Just a group of a hundred cells rapidly multiplying. The inner layer of cells will develop into the embryo, the outer layer into the placenta.
2 weeks	About the size of the head of a pin. There is now the beginning of a face, with a mouth opening and dark circles where the eyes will be. A heart has started to develop, as has a brain. And because the spinal cord grows at a faster rate than the rest of the body, at this stage the baby also has a tail.
4 weeks	The heart is now beating. The buds of the limbs begin to form, as do the beginnings of the eyes.
6 weeks	The arms continue to grow and now bend at the elbow. The larynx starts to form. The tip of the nose is visible.
8 weeks	The hands have fingers and the feet have toes. The eyes have developed, although the eyelids remain sealed shut. A nose and a tongue are beginning to form. All the major organs are now present, and the baby is able to make spontaneous movements.
12 weeks	Weighs about 1½ ounces and is about 3 inches long – that is, approximately the size of an orange. A neck has developed. Fingers and toes now have nails. There are taste buds inside the mouth, and also evidence of a sucking reflex. The twenty buds that will one day be baby teeth are discernible.
16 weeks	Weighs about 5 ounces and is about 5 inches long. The ears have moved up from the neck to the head, and the baby now has fingerprints and toeprints. Also able to suck thumb and practise breathing. Arms and legs can be seen to move. Will startle at loud noises. In a baby girl, the uterus has formed and the ovaries contain egg cells.

22 weeks	Weighs about ½ pound and is about 8 inches long. Able to do somersaults. Ears are well developed enough to recognize sound. The face has expressions: for example, the baby is able to frown. Has hair on the head and also the eyebrows. In a baby boy, the testicles have started to descend from the abdomen into the scrotum.
26 weeks	Weighs about 2 pounds and is about 1 foot long. Able to pedal feet and grip with hands. Vocal cords work. Eyes open and close and react to light, so that if a very bright light is shone at the mother's stomach, the baby can be seen to shield its eyes in protest.
30 weeks	Weighs about 3 pounds and is about 16 inches long. Eyebrows and eyelashes now fully grown. Lungs beginning to function. The brain is growing at a very rapid rate.
34 weeks	Weighs about 5–6 pounds and is about 18 inches long. Lungs now fully mature. The brain continues to grow.
38 weeks	Now considered full term. The baby gets settled into position – most commonly head down – ready to be born.

NHS ETIQUETTE FOR BEGINNERS

WHILE one wouldn't wish to denigrate the sacred and civilized institution that is our great National Health Service, it is important to maintain realistic expectations of its capacity and potential. Although ambitiously and admirably hopeful of providing every expectant mother with levels of ante- and post-natal care to rival that of private institutions, it obviously can't. However, ways exist of garnering the sort of respect from medical professionals that is guaranteed to ease your (and your baby's) passage through the crowded corridors of the state maternity unit.

Once the sixth home pregnancy test has confirmed that yes, conception has indeed occurred, make an appointment with the GP. Wear something demure and neat. Present yourself in a contained, non-hysterical fashion, regardless of the state of inner turmoil. The GP has a hotline to social services, and you don't want to start alarm bells ringing. At the surgery, instructions will be issued about riding a bike (which can still happen) and using a sauna (which cannot). The question may then be posed, depending on your geographical location: which hospital? For many pregnant ladies, there is just the one to choose from: the nearest, or only, local maternity unit. However, if you live in a racy metropolis, it is your Right to Choose the place lucky enough to deliver your precious progeny. The GP may attempt to persuade, or bias, your decision – perhaps GPs receive extra stethoscopes if they succeed in evenly populating city hospitals – but stick to your guns. Thoroughly research which institution boasts the best canteen, as well as grounds in which you can pleasantly picture yourself stomping around (moaning primitively) in nine months' time, and that has to be the place for you.

The NHS midwife

You will soon be assigned a midwife and assured she will make contact. She may not. If she does, you may have to take the morning off work to attend the surgery at her convenience. Only to find that it was clearly not all that convenient, for she hasn't attended herself. At this point (your sickest, yet you are unable to tell work why the morning off was required), you may justifiably give up and decide to have the baby on the kitchen floor. Or perhaps you will be lucky, and receive continuity of care to rival that of England in the 1950s, with a lone, doting lady practitioner elegantly chaperoning you through your every backache, yeast infection and scan. If not, take the view that anything good is worth fighting for. Make polite but insistent phone calls, until a sort of quirkily cut jigsaw puzzle of maternity treatment begins to take form around you. Once granted a face-to-face, try to use complex medical terms well (possibly even in Latin). This will demonstrate that you have read widely on the Internet, and are no soft touch.

The NHS hospital

You will attend the hospital for scans, and for excruciating workshops on breastfeeding, pain relief and how to use cloth nappies. There will be a faint odour of assorted bodily effluent, as well as a pronounced odour of alcoholic hand sanitizer, a persistent number of non-uniformed staff slopping about in an Eeyore-like manner and lots of blood tests. Again, treat everyone in a patient, mildly condescending manner, more than vaguely suggestive of a Ph.D. in a probably relevant area of obstetric medicine. And watch the results! The glint of stainless steel, boasting properties reminiscent of a piece of gynaecological equipment, nonchalantly peeking from the back pocket of your maternity jeans may assist with this impression.

Whatever sort of birth you plan, plan for it not to be this way. One thing you *can* plan, however, is your warm-up outfit. Keeping it free-at-the-point-of-delivery does not mean delivery itself has to get all slouchy. Perk up yoga-type basics with a jaunty fluoro headband or polka-dot vest top (if one can be found large enough to encircle your elephantine bulk). While in labour, implement the now well-practised, mildly patronizing, seen-it-all strategy with visiting consultants and, in spite of any discomfort, do attempt to smile wearily at the vast numbers of students that will surge in and stare up you. The best way of dealing with this degree of dignity deficit is to make out that this position (whatever it might be) and this strange level of nudity (with any luck, you will have managed to hang on to the perky headband) is currently the *only* way to be papped. At this stage, conceal the possibly gynaecological tool you have been transporting to antenatal consultations. An over-zealous student may seize it and attempt to apply it to you, before realizing too late that it was part of a household blender.

ROMAN GODDESSES

Alemona	*Protects the health and safety of the baby while still in the womb.*
Camoena	*Teaches children to sing.*
Candelifera	*A goddess of childbirth. Helps the baby emerge into the light of the world. Her name means 'candle-bearer'.*
Carmentia	*Another goddess of childbirth. Thought to prophesy the baby's destiny. Her name is derived from the word 'carmen', meaning 'oracle'.*
Cuba	*Helps babies sleep. Particularly worth making friends with, then.*
Cunina	*Guards the baby's cradle.*
Dea Mens	*In charge of the child's mind and consciousness.*
Deverra	*Protects the new mother and baby by driving evil spirits from wherever the baby was born.*
Edusa	*A goddess of nourishment. Watches over the baby's first solid foods.*
Fabulinus	*Governs the first words uttered.*
Lucina	*Another goddess of childbirth. As the goddess of moonlight too, she is the source of the first light seen by a newborn. Helps opens a baby's eyes for the first time. When invoking her during labour to ease the pain, worshippers used to unpin their hair and untie any knots in their clothing to symbolize allowing the energy to flow.*
Partula	*Another goddess of childbirth. Determines the duration of the pregnancy.*
Pilumnus	*Guards the baby at the moment it is delivered.*
Potina	*Another goddess of nourishment. Watches over the baby's first drink from a cup.*
Rumina	*The goddess of breastfeeding.*
Vagitanus	*Watches over the first sound a baby makes when it is born.*
Volumna	*The goddess of the nursery.*

ZZZZZZZZZZZZZZZZ

A cot, a travel cot, a co-sleeper, in your bed, on your chest, in the car seat being driven around all night: like much in the modern world, the choice of sleeping arrangements for your baby is overwhelming, and yet one that obsesses many of us during pregnancy. An option that has been popular for centuries is the Moses basket. On this, see the 1976 classic of the genre, *The Pauper's Homemaking Book* by Jocasta Innes. 'I don't suppose an infant notices whether it sleeps in an orange box or a nest of frills,' she writes, 'so long as its chief needs are attended to. But mothers, even the most anti-frill in the ordinary way, feel an impulse to surround a new baby with soft, pretty, beribboned things.' Innes goes on to instruct the reader at great length, in a passage that is a masterpiece of 1970s period detail with its various references to terylene and polyester, on how to decorate a Moses basket oneself.

For the baby-basket, you will need a wickerwork crib, or soft straw Moses basket with two handles . . . The next requirement is a cotton fabric for the lining . . . Choose a washable, pretty cotton rather than nylon or Terylene; gingham in tiny checks, violet, perhaps, as a compromise between pink and blue, or a small floral print . . . It is a sensible precaution to wash the cotton lining fabric before sewing it, to prevent it from shrinking later. Iron it smooth when damp. Cut a pattern from newspaper or large sheets of paper, Sellotaped where they need to be joined. It is easier to machine-quilt smallish sections at a time, so make the lining for the sides of the basket in two sections, seamed together at head and foot. The lining should come to just below the wickerwork rim of a crib, or the edge of the carrying basket. Add on 1 inch all round to allow for turn-backs and seams. Cut a pattern for the base in the same way, with a 1-inch seam-allowance. Cut two pieces of lining fabric and wadding for the sides of the basket, and a piece of lining fabric only for the base. (When joined up the pieces will be something like a large bag with quilted sides.) Tack the side sections to the wadding, criss-crossing the lines of tacking so as to hold the fabric and wadding together securely while you machine-quilt. Quilt each side-section separately using a strong matching thread, cotton or Polyester for choice. The lines of machine-quilting can go in any direction you fancy, in parallel rows round the basket sides or, perhaps prettier, in a diagonal trellis pattern. Right sides together, tack the sections together at each end. Then tack the lining for the base to the quilted sides, pinning it in place first to check that it is the right size. Try the lining in the basket to see whether it needs to be made any smaller to fit smoothly. Make any adjustments needed, then machine the pieces together . . .

Oh, forget it. Anyone who actually perseveres to the end deserves a medal.

Furthermore, the trouble with a Moses basket is that it looks sweet but gets used for only about five minutes until the baby grows out of it. Many swear by some sort of contraption that can easily be rocked — a pram, a cradle or even a cot to which wheels have been attached — for it is no accident that once upon a time, rich households employed a nursemaid known as the Rocker solely to perform this soul-destroying task. Aaah, those were the days. A better option might be a travel cot that comes with a bassinette feature: these are a little tricky to track down but do exist, and are a fantastic investment because once the baby grows out of it, which, as with a Moses basket is pretty quickly, it can be used as a regular travel cot for an older baby, or even as a playpen. Alternatively, you could even have the baby sleep in a drawer lined with sheepskin, as mothers have done throughout history. Just be sure not to close the drawer absentmindedly whilst ferreting around for a dropped earring.

A QUIZ TO HELP YOU DETERMINE THE SEX OF YOUR BABY

	A	B
How are you carrying the baby?	Low	High
How are you carrying the extra weight?	Out front	In your hips and bottom
What is the baby's heart rate?	Less than 140 beats per minute	More than 140 beats per minute
What do you crave?	Sour or salty food, or protein	Sweet food or fruit
Has your partner put on weight during your pregnancy?	Yes	No
Which of your breasts is currently larger?	The right one	The left one
If you dangle a pendant over your stomach, how does it swing?	Back and forth	In circles
Did you have morning sickness in the early stages of your pregnancy?	No	Yes

	A	B
Are your feet chillier than usual?	Yes	No
Are your hands drier than usual?	Yes	No
What colour is your urine?	Bright yellow	Dull yellow
Have your areolae got darker?	Yes	No
How do you look?	Better than ever	Worse than ever
Are you getting headaches?	Yes	No
Have you developed red highlights in your hair?	No	Yes
Are you getting more acne than usual?	No	Yes
What direction does your pillow face when you sleep?	North	South
Has the hair on your legs grown faster than usual?	Yes	No
If you add your age when the baby was conceived to the number of the month during which you conceived, what is the resulting figure?	Even	Odd

If you score mostly As, you are having a boy. If you score mostly Bs, you are having a girl. All this is entirely unscientific, of course, and based on folklore – some of it crazy, some of it not quite so crazy. Of all the methods, the most reliable seems to be whether you are carrying the baby high or low. This is the one that complete strangers accost you with in the street, touching your stomach in an entirely inappropriate and intrusive way, all the while insisting on informing you of the sex of your unborn baby, therefore ruining the surprise completely even before your twenty-week scan, darn it.

EDD ETC.; OR, A GUIDE TO SOME COMMON MEDICAL ABBREVIATIONS

Pregnancy

20+3:	length of pregnancy, expressed as number of weeks plus days	gest:	gestation
		GTT:	glucose tolerance test
		HBP:	high blood pressure
AGA:	appropriate gestational age	IUP:	intrauterine pregnancy
		LBP:	lower-back pain
amnio:	amniocentesis	LGA:	large for gestational age
AP:	antepartum	LMP:	last menstrual period
CBC:	complete blood count	MH:	marital history
cnst:	constipation	MSU:	midstream urine sample
D&C:	dilation and curettage	NAD:	no apparent distress
D&E:	dilation and evacuation	N&V:	nausea and vomiting
DUB:	dysfunctional uterine bleeding	Para:	prior births (para0 = no prior births, para1 = 1 prior birth, etc.)
EDD:	estimated due date		
FEKG:	foetal electrocardiogram	plac:	placenta
FHR:	foetal heart rate	PMH:	past medical history
FMF:	foetal movements felt	PU:	pregnancy urine
FUB:	functional uterine bleeding	US, u/s:	ultrasound
		ut:	uterus, uterine
FW:	foetal weight	VE:	vaginal examination

1/5–5/5: indicated extent of head engagement

AROM: artificial rupture of membranes

Br: breech presentation

BW: birth weight

CB: Caesarean birth

Ceph: cephalic presentation (i.e. the baby is positioned head down)

cont: contractions

C/S: Caesarean section

Ctx: contractions

ELF: elective low forceps

eng: engaged (i.e. the baby's head has dropped into the pelvis)

epis: episiotomy

FD: fully dilated

FHT: foetal heart tones

FT: full term

FTD: failure to descend

FTND: full-term normal delivery

FTP: failure to progress

GA: general anaesthesia

L&D: labour and delivery

LBW: low birth weight

LOA: left occipital anterior (i.e. the back of the baby's head is forward on your left)

LOL: left occipital longitudinal lie (i.e. the baby is lying sideways with the head on your left)

LOP: left occipital posterior (i.e. the back of the baby's head is backwards on your left)

LSCS: lower-segment Caesarean section

NB: newborn

NE: not engaged

p/e, p-e: pre-eclampsia

ROA: right occipital anterior (i.e. the back of the baby's head is forward on your right)

ROL: right occipital longitudinal lie (i.e. the baby is lying sideways with the head on your right)

ROP: right occipital posterior (i.e. the back of the baby's head is backwards on your right)

RUC: regular uterine contraction

SROM: spontaneous rupture of membranes (i.e. your water breaking). Also . . . AROM: artificial rupture of membranes

Syn: syntocin. Also known as Pit: pitocin.

UC: uterine contractions

VTX, Vx: vertex presentation

ORAL SEX

FOR many pregnant women, the prospect of sex in the conventional sense becomes progressively less appealing – even (dare one say it?) progressively more repellent – as the months go by. There is, however, no ailment yet invented that precludes oral sex. And if you are going to do it, you might as well do it to the very best of your ability, with unparalleled vim and vigour, for Queen and country. So with this in mind, let us turn to the *Kama Sutra*, a Sanskrit text written by Mallanāga Vātsyāyana in the second century, for advice.

As she massages the man, she caresses his two thighs with her limbs, as if she were embracing him. Then she becomes more boldly intimate and familiar and touches the places where his thighs join his torso, and his sexual organ. If she notices that he has become hard as a result of this, she stimulates him by using her hand as a churn, pretending to tease him about how easily he becomes excited and laughing at him. If the man does not urge her on, even when he has given this clear sign and even when it is obvious that he is aroused, she makes advances to him on her own. If the man urges her to go on, she argues with him and only unwillingly continues.

Oral sex involves eight acts, one after the other:

- Casual
- Biting The Sides
- The Outer Tongs
- The Inner Tongs

- Kissing
- Polishing
- Sucking The Mango
- Swallowing

As she finishes each one, she expresses her wish to stop, and when each one is finished, the man asks her to do the next one, and when that is finished, the one after that. In the 'Casual' act, she holds it with her hand, places it on her lips, pierces her mouth with it and moves it back and forth. She bares the glans with her hand, nibbles at its sides with her two lips, keeping her teeth away, and she tantalises him by saying, 'This is as far as I go.' That is 'Biting The Sides'. When the man urges her to do more, she closes her lips. Presses them down on the glans and kisses him as if drawing it out. That is called 'The Outer Tongs'. Begging her to go on doing this, he pushes a little deeper into her mouth, and she squeezes the glans with her lips and then spits it out. That is called 'The Inner Tongs.' Then she holds it in her hand and grasps it as if it were his lip. That is 'Kissing'. After she has done that, she licks it all over with the top of her tongue and then pierces the glans. That is called 'Polishing'. When it is in precisely this state, driven halfway inside her mouth through the force of passion, she mercilessly presses down, and presses down again, and lets it go. That is called 'Sucking The Mango'. Only when the man asks for it does she swallow it up and press until the climax. That is called 'Swallowing.' Groaning and slapping may also be used, as they are called for.

THE WORLD'S LONGEST FILMS – BECAUSE IT'S NOW OR NEVER

Title	Year released	Length
Berlin Alexanderplatz	1980	15 hours 31 minutes
Resan (The Journey)	1987	14 hours 33 minutes
Out 1: Noli me tangere*	1971	12 hours 53 minutes
How Yukong Moved the Mountains	1977	12 hours 43 minutes
Evolution of a Filipino Family	2004	10 hours 43 minutes
Shoah	1985	9 hours 26 minutes
Tie Xi Qu: West of the Tracks	2003	9 hours 16 minutes
Heremias Book One: The Legend of the Lizard Princess	2006	9 hours
Death in the Land of the Encantos	2007	9 hours
Taiga	1992	8 hours 21 minutes
Liberation	1969	8 hours 7 minutes
War and Peace†	1968	8 hours 4 minutes
The Photo-Drama of Creation	1914	8 hours
El Protegido de Satán	1917	8 hours
Imitation of Christ	1967	8 hours

---

* Directed by Jacques Rivette (b. 1928), a French film critic who later moved into directing and was at the centre of the French New Wave movement along with the likes of Jean-Luc Godard and François Truffaut. His best-known film is probably the 1974 classic *Céline et Julie Vont En Bateau* (Céline and Julie Go Boating) in which the two title characters chance upon a strange mansion in the centre of Paris where every single day plays out in exactly the same way. A bit like spending a week home alone with a small baby, then.

† This version of *War and Peace* took seven years to produce and cost over $100 million – which, adjusted for inflation, makes it the most expensive film ever made. One of the battle scenes featured 120,000 extras recruited from the Soviet army and real weapons raided from military museums all over the USSR. In 1968 it won an Oscar for the Best Foreign Language Film. The film is also notable for being one of the few epics not to have originated in Hollywood.

Title	Year released	Length
Melancholia	2008	8 hours
Mefisto	1917	7 hours 40 minutes
Satantango	1994	7 hours 30 minutes
Hitler: A Film from Germany	1978	7 hours 22 minutes
Arshin Mal Alan	1916	7 hours
The Satin Slipper	1985	6 hours 50 minutes
Bábolna	1985	6 hours 40 minutes
The Best of Youth	2003	6 hours 40 minutes
I, Paisan	1967	6 hours 32 minutes
Parisette	1921	6 hours 20 minutes
Babel: A Letter to My Friends Left Behind in Belgium	1991	6 hours 20 minutes
The Stand	1994	6 hours 6 minutes
Little Dorrit	1988	6 hours
La Révolution Française	1989	6 hours
Bevezetés a Filmkészítés Rejtelmeibe	1996	6 hours
Les Misérables	1925	5 hours 59 minutes
The Fight for Moscow	1985	5 hours 58 minutes
Near Death	1989	5 hours 58 minutes
Fragments: Jerusalem	1997	5 hours 58 minutes
La Commune (Paris, 1871)	2000	5 hours 45 minutes
And Quiet Flows the Don	1957–8	5 hours 40 minutes
Perón, Sinfonía del Sentimiento	1999	5 hours 40 minutes
L'Idole des Jeunes	1976	5 hours 38 minutes
Vkus Khleba	1979	5 hours 36 minutes
Napoléon	1927	5 hours 30 minutes
Mahatma: Life of Gandhi, 1869–1948	1968	5 hours 30 minutes
Yoman	1983	5 hours 30 minutes

Title	Year released	Length
Spiritual Voices	1995	5 hours 28 minutes
Vindicta	1923	5 hours 20 minutes
*Cleopatra**	1963	5 hours 20 minutes
As I Was Moving Ahead Occasionally I Saw Brief Glimpses of Beauty	2000	5 hours 20 minutes
1900	1976	5 hours 18 minutes
The Deluge	1974	5 hours 16 minutes
Tsahal	1994	5 hours 16 minutes
Batang West Side	2002	5 hours 15 minutes
Nightmare	1972	5 hours 12 minutes
Fanny and Alexander	1983	5 hours 12 minutes
Legend About Thiel	1976	5 hours 11 minutes
Les Misérables	1934	5 hours 5 minutes
The Confessions of Winifred Wagner	1975	5 hours 2 minutes

* It was on the set of *Cleopatra* that Elizabeth Taylor embarked on her great romance with Richard Burton. In Burton's autobiography, *Meeting Mrs. Jenkins* (1966), he describes the moment he first set eyes on her, which was at a party in Bel Air:

> [A] girl sitting on the other side of the pool lowered her book, took off her sunglasses, and looked at me. She was so extraordinarily beautiful that I nearly laughed out loud. She . . . [was] famine, fire, destruction and plague . . . the only true begetter. Her breasts were apocalyptic, they would topple empires down before they withered. Indeed, her body was a miracle of construction and the work of an engineer of genius. It needed nothing but itself. It was true art, I thought, executed in terms of itself. It was smitten by its own passion . . . She was lavish. She was a dark, unyielding largesse. She was, in short, too bloody much . . . Aeons passed, civilizations came and went while these cosmic headlights examined my flawed personality. Every pockmark on my face became a crater of the moon.

But even a romance of this magnitude could not sustain through the vagaries of marriage and then the adoption of a little girl from Germany, and in 1976 Taylor and Burton divorced for the second and final time.

THE GESTATION PERIOD OF ANIMALS

THE huge majority of babies born in Britain – 88 per cent, according to NHS statistics – are delivered between 37 and 41 weeks, with 28 per cent taking the conventional 40 weeks to ready themselves. There are always exceptions, however: 7 per cent are delivered before 37 weeks and 4.2 per cent after 42 weeks, including 70 babies who took an astonishing 48 weeks to decide they wanted to emerge into the big wide world (although in at least some of these cases, one suspects some confusion over the due date). The gestation period of humans would be longer were it not for the need for the human brain to fit through a pelvis that, with evolution, has become progressively narrower in order to allow us to walk upright, rather than on all fours. As a result, the human brain is not fully developed by the end of the 40 weeks; note, for example, that deer can run as soon as they are born, whereas it takes human babies another year or so to reach this stage. This is why some refer to the first few months of a baby's life as the fourth trimester. No wonder babies often seem a bit depressed to be so rudely ejected from the warm, dark confines of the womb: they are really not developmentally ready yet.

The mother, on the other hand, is very often *more* than ready by the time 40 weeks have passed. So pity the Indian elephant, which has the longest known gestation period in the animal kingdom: the average is 660 days, up to a maximum of 760 days. Sorry, 760 *days*? That's over two years. The shortest gestation period is 12–13 days, a record shared by three marsupials (whose young finish developing in a pouch located near the mother's abdomen): the Virginian opossum, the rare water opossum and the eastern quoll.

The length of the gestation period is determined by a number of factors, among them the animal's natural habitat. Animals living out in the open gestate for longer, and thus give birth to more fully developed offspring, than those living in caves or burrows, which provide shelter. Among species with limited breeding seasons, the birth occurs whenever food is at its most plentiful. So the horse, which mates in spring, gestates for 11 months and then delivers the following spring; the sheep mates in autumn, gestates for 5 months and then delivers in spring. Larger animals usually have longer gestation periods than smaller ones, and there are also variations within this depending on the sex: a bull averages a day longer than a heifer, a human male 3–4 days longer than a human female.

AVERAGE GESTATION PERIODS

Anteater	190 days	Dog	63 days
Bat	46–70 days	Dolphin	270–350 days
Beaver	100–110 days	Donkey	275 days
Budgerigar	18 days	Duck	28 days
Camel	406 days	Elephant (African)	540–700 days
Cat	63 days	Elephant (Indian)	600–760 days
Cheetah	90–95 days	Ferret	42 days
Chicken	22 days	Fox	53 days
Chimpanzee	202–261 days	Gerbil	25 days
Chinchilla	111 days	Giraffe	400–450 days
Cow	280 days	Goat	150 days

Groundhog	32 days	Orang-utan	275 days
Guinea pig	68 days	Otter	62 days
Hamster	16 days	Pig	115 days
Hedgehog	30–40 days	Pigeon	11–19 days
Hippopotamus	240 days	Polar bear	240 days
Horse	336 days	Puma	91 days
Human	280 days	Rabbit	31 days
Hyena	110 days	Raccoon	60–73 days
Jaguar	110 days	Rat	21 days
Kangaroo	31–39 days	Reindeer	215–245 days
Lemming	21 days	Sheep	150 days
Lion	105–110 days	Skunk	70 days
Llama	331–367 days	Squirrel	44 days
Mink	50 days	Tiger	104–112 days
Monkey	139–270 days	Weasel	35 days
Moose	240–270 days	Whale	365–540 days
Mouse	19–24 days	Wolf	62 days
Opossum	12–13 days	Zebra	360–390 days

A PREGNANT BODY AT FORTY WEEKS

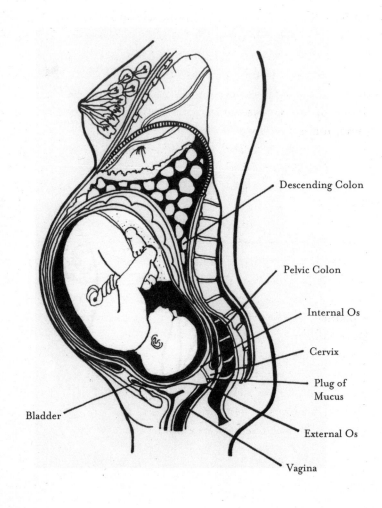

Descending Colon

Pelvic Colon

Internal Os

Cervix

Plug of Mucus

Bladder

External Os

Vagina

GIN RUMMY

LIKE an Ibsen play or the Hundred Years War, the ninth month of pregnancy often feels downright interminable. So why not make those seconds tick by a little faster by mastering the art of gin rummy? It is the perfect way to pass the time during those last, long evenings when one is too tired even to dream of leaving the hephalump house. A two-person card game, it also merrily occupies one's paramour, whose fear of his missus going into labour is matched only by the fear that he will be roaringly drunk when she does; hence he tends to spend a lot of time twiddling his thumbs too, trying not to reach for the liquor bottle.

Gin rummy was invented in Brooklyn in 1909, but only really became popular in the 1940s when Hollywood caught on to its appeal. In 1960, it had the honour of featuring in what is officially The World's Greatest Film, Billy Wilder's *The Apartment*. As one of the film's stars, Shirley MacLaine, explained, 'At the time I was hanging with Frank [Sinatra] and Dean [Martin], learning how to play Gin Rummy. (That's why the gin game is in the apartment.)' The result is the film's classic final line: 'Shut up and deal!' retorts MacLaine's character, Fran, when Jack Lemmon's character, C.C. Baxter, declares his love for her. And so its status as the chicest card game in town was fixed for ever.

Taking turns in each round, a player deals out ten cards to herself (or himself) and ten cards to her opponent. The twenty-first card is then placed on the table face up (this is known as the upcard), and all the remaining cards are placed on the table next to it in a pile face down (this is known as the discard).

The aim of the game is to reach a state where all the cards one holds in one's hand are either a run (that is, three cards or more of the same suit in a row, e.g. a 3 of hearts, a 4 of hearts and a 5 of hearts) or a set (that is, three cards or more of the same rank, e.g. a 3 of hearts, a 3 of clubs and a 3 of spades).

Each time a player has a turn, she has one of two options. She can choose to take the upcard, or she can take her chances, sight unseen, with whatever card is on the top of the discard pile.

The player then has to choose which one of her cards to get rid of. This becomes the new upcard, and so the game continues.

For the purposes of scoring, an ace is 1 point, a two is 2 points and so on, with a Jack, a Queen and a King all valued at 10 points. The round finishes when a player finds herself with less than 10 points' worth of dead wood, at which point she may choose to 'knock', which signals the end of a round. Alternatively, when one player has no points left in her hand that are not in a run or a set, she is obliged to knock; this is known as going Gin.

- The aim should always be to create two sets, plus four or fewer unattached cards of low value. It is rare to make three sets.
- Keep track of which cards have been discarded, and hence which sets are worth pursuing. This is the key to success.
- Look for 7s. A 7 is the most useful card in the game because it features in more combinations than any other card. The least useful? The King and the Ace.
- Knock as soon as possible. It is rare to make Gin, so just go for the points.

CURRY

OLD wives' tales abound about how to induce a baby. In this lady author's opinion, acupuncture is the safest, most effective method. If acupuncture is not an option, because of constraints temporal, financial or otherwise, the methods that hearsay suggests have the highest success rates are drinking raspberry leaf tea (hard to buy), having sex (hard to bear) or eating curry. So curry it is, then. Here are some of the most popular kinds.

Bhuna

Technically a method of cooking rather than a dish. The spices are cooked in hot oil to create a dryish but deeply flavoured curry. Usually includes coconut too.

Dhansak

Originally a Persian dish combining elements of Persian and Gujarati cuisine, this is distinguished by the presence of lots of lentils in a sauce that is at the same time hot (chilli), sweet (usually sugar, occasionally pineapple) and sour (lemon juice).

Dopiaza

Prepare to eat a lot of onions when ordering this dish. Dopiaza translates from Urdu as 'two onions' or 'double onions'. These are added both early on to the sauce and then again towards the end of the cooking process. Medium hot.

Jalfrezi

Like bhuna, jalfrezi is technically a method of cooking rather than a dish: jalfrezi translates as 'hot fry'. A dry, thick sauce with tomatoes, green peppers and green chillies that in terms of taste tends to be on the hotter side. Traditionally used with leftover meat, and highly spiced to disguise the fact that the meat was on the turn.

Korma

The korma that is served in British curry houses — rich, mild, creamy, with almonds or cashews and usually yellowish in colour — bears little relation to its Mughal predecessor, which was named after the Hindi and Urdu word for 'braise'.

Madras

A hotter version of a regular curry that was invented by British curry houses. Usually contains extra chilli, lemon juice, almonds and tomatoes.

Moghlai

The key ingredients are ginger, almonds, yoghurt and cream. Mild to medium.

Pasanda	*From the Urdu word* **pasande**, *meaning 'favourite one' – referring to the quality of the meat traditionally used in this dish. Also contains cardamom, almonds, tomatoes and cream.*
Rogan josh	*In Persian,* **rogan** *means oil and* **josh** *means heat. It is distinguished by its deep red colour, which comes from the use of ground red chillies, red peppers and/or tomatoes. Paprika is also sometimes added. Medium hot.*
Saag	*A curry cooked bhuna-style with any kind of green leaf such as spinach or fenugreek. Medium hot.*
Tikka masala	*Ingredients vary considerably, but tikka masala generally consists of some sort of tomato-y, creamy sauce. To look at, it is usually bright red, though this is more often due to the addition of artificial food colouring than anything else.*
Vindaloo	*Derives from the Portuguese dish Carne de Vinha d'Alhos, which early Portuguese settlers brought with them to Goa in India in the seventeenth century. It is now most British curry restaurants' standard super-hot dish, and thus most certainly not to be recommended for a pregnant woman, however overdue she might be.*

This is in addition, of course, to all the varieties of Thai curry, Vietnamese curry and the multitude of other hot messes on offer.

BABY, OH BABY

English	Baby	Japanese	赤ちゃん
Afrikaans	Baby	Korean	아기
Albanian	Foshnjë	Latvian	Mazulis
Arabic	لفط	Lithuanian	Vaikas
Belarusian	дзіця	Macedonian	бебе
Bulgarian	бебе	Malay	Bayi
Catalan	Nadó	Maltese	Tarbija
Chinese	婴儿	Norwegian	Baby
Croatian	Beba	Persian	ضزاد
Czech	Dítě	Polish	Niemowlę
Danish	Baby	Portuguese	Bebê
Dutch	Baby	Romanian	copil
Estonian	Laps	Russian	ребенок
Filipino	Sanggol	Serbian	беба
Finnish	Vauva	Slovak	Diet'a
French	Bébé	Slovenian	Dojen
Galician	Bebé	Spanish	Bebé
German	Baby	Swahili	Mtoto
Greek	Μωρό	Swedish	Bebis
Hebrew	קונית	Thai	ทารก
Hindi	हिड्डा	Turkish	Bebek
Hungarian	Baba	Ukrainian	дитина
Icelandic	Barnið	Vietnamese	đứa bé
Indonesian	Bayi	Welsh	Babi
Irish	Leanbh	Yiddish	עפׂוע
Italian	Bambino		

BIRTH IN THE UK: THE NUMBERS

Year	Number of live births	Fertility rate (average number of children per woman aged 15–44)	Sex ratio (live male births per 1,000 live female births)	Mean age of mother at childbirth	Percentage of live births outside marriage	Percentage of live births to non-UK-born mothers
1998	635,901	1.72	1,051	28.3	37.8	13.6
1999	621,872	1.70	1,055	28.4	38.9	14.3
2000	604,441	1.65	1,050	28.5	39.5	15.5
2001	594,634	1.63	1,050	28.6	40.0	16.5
2002	596,122	1.65	1,055	28.7	40.6	17.7
2003	621,469	1.73	1,051	28.8	41.4	18.6
2004	639,721	1.78	1,054	28.9	42.2	19.5
2005	645,835	1.79	1,049	29.1	42.8	20.8
2006	669,601	1.86	1,047	29.1	43.5	21.9
2007	690,013	1.92	1,057	29.3	44.3	23.2
2008	708,711	1.97 (the highest rate since 1973)	1,050	29.3	45.3	24.1

Source: Office of National Statistics

AN EXTRACT FROM THE AUTOBIOGRAPHY OF BENAZIR BHUTTO, WHO WAS NOT ONLY TWICE PRIME MINISTER OF PAKISTAN BUT ALSO THE FIRST LEADER OF A MODERN STATE TO GIVE BIRTH WHILE IN OFFICE

I am grateful to my mother for teaching me that pregnancy is a biological state of being which should not disrupt the normal routine of life. Trying to live up to her expectations, I almost ignored any hint of physical or emotional limitation during my pregnancies. Yet I was acutely conscious that what should have been a family matter became a topic of intense political discussion from military headquarters to editorial boards. Aware of this, I kept the exact details of my pregnancies secret.

I have three lovely children: Bilawal, Bakhtwar and Aseefa. They give me much joy and pride. When I was expecting my first child, Bilawal, in 1988, I was 35, and the then military dictator dismissed the parliament and called for general elections. He and his top army men believed a pregnant woman could not campaign. They were wrong. I could and I did. I went on to win the elections held shortly after Bilawal's birth on September 21 1988. Bilawal's birth was one of the happiest days of my life. Winning those elections that year, despite predictions that a Muslim woman could not win the hearts and minds of her people, was another.

Shortly after I was elected prime minister, my mother told me to 'hurry up and have another child'. She believed that a mother should quickly have children before she realised the challenges of raising a family and fulfilling other responsibilities. I took her advice.

Once the political opposition learned I was pregnant, all hell broke loose. They called on the president and the military to overthrow me. They argued that Pakistan's government rules did not provide for a pregnant prime minister going on maternity leave. They said that during delivery I would be incapacitated and therefore the government machinery would irretrievably break down for that period of time. This, to them, was unconstitutional, necessitating the president, backed by the military, to dismiss the prime minister and install an interim government to hold new elections.

I rejected the opposition's demands, noting that maternity rules existed in the law for working women (my father had legislated maternity leave). I argued that the law implicitly applied to a prime minister even if not stated in the rules for conducting government business. The members of my government stood by me, noting that when a male leader was indisposed, it did not translate into a constitutional crisis. Nor should it were a female leader indisposed.

Hardly mollified, the opposition drew up a plan of strikes to pressure the president into sacking the government. I had to make my own plans.

My father had taught me that in politics, timing is very important. I consulted my doctor who assured me that my child was full term and, with his permission, decided to have a Caesarean delivery on the eve of the call for strike action.

I didn't want to encourage any stereotypes that pregnancy interferes with performance. So, despite my condition, I worked just as hard, and probably a lot harder, than a male prime minister would have done. In the end, I chaired a meeting of my cabinet in the capital and then left for Karachi. I woke up early in the morning and with a friend left for the hospital in her car.

It was a small car, very different from the black Mercedes used for official duties. The police on security duty hardly gave it a second glance. They concentrated on cars entering my home rather than those leaving it.

My heart was beating fast as we raced to the hospital, where my doctor was waiting for us. I could see the surprise on the faces of the hospital staff as I got out of the car. I knew the news would begin to spread fast through the mobile phones and pagers that my government had introduced (we were the first country in South Asia and the Middle East to have mobile phones).

I hurried down the hallway to the operating theatre. I knew that my husband and mother would be on their way, as we had discussed earlier. As soon as I began to wake from the mists of anaesthesia as my hospital trolley was wheeled from the theatre to the private room, I heard my husband say: 'It's a girl.' I saw my mother's face beam with pleasure. I called my daughter Bakhtwar, which means the one who brings good fortune. And she did. The strikes fizzled out and the opposition's movement collapsed.

I received thousands of messages of congratulations from all over the world. Heads of government and ordinary people wrote to me, sharing the joy. It was a defining moment, especially for young women, proving a woman could work and have a baby in the highest and most challenging leadership positions. The next day I was back on the job, reading government papers and signing government files. Only later did I learn that I was the only head of government in recorded history actually to give birth while in office.

Bakhtwar was born in January 1990 . . . [then, in August 1990, Bhutto was dismissed from office by the President of Pakistan.]

In the spring of 1992 I found I was expecting another baby. As one of four children, it gave me great pleasure to know our family would grow . . . [Yet] I began suffering from gall-bladder pain. I took homeopathic medicine but the pain continued. It was often excruciating. If I had an operation to fix it, I risked losing my child. I didn't want to take the risk. As the pain got worse and worse, I flew to London. The doctors advised that I should have a Caesarean as soon as possible, followed by keyhole surgery to remove the gall bladder. On February 3 1993, my little daughter Aseefa was born. I cuddled my adorable little baby.*

Benazir Bhutto, *Daughter of the East* (2007)

---

* In October 1993, Bhutto was elected Prime Minister of Pakistan for the second time, a position she held until November 1996. Eleven years later, while campaigning on behalf of the Pakistan People's Party in the city of Rawalpindi, she was assassinated.

SIGNS OF THE ZODIAC

Latin name	English name	Symbol	Dates	Brightest star	Ruled by which planet?	Ruled by which element?	Personality traits
Aries	The Ram	♈	20 March–20 April	Hamal	Mars	Fire	A natural leader, ambitious, bossy, energetic, determined, impatient, organized, enthusiastic, optimistic, argumentative, headstrong, aggressive, easily bored, impulsive, adventurous
Taurus	The Bull	♉	20 April–21 May	Aldebaran	Venus	Earth	Dependable, patient, reliable, determined, methodical, careful, good listener, a people pleaser, stubborn, possessive
Gemini	The Twins	♊	21 May–21 June	Pollux	Mercury	Air	Adaptable, good at making friends, life of the party, restless, curious, fun, talkative, communicative, inquisitive
Cancer	The Crab	♋	21 June–22 July	Al Tarf	Moon	Water	Easy-going, sympathetic, sensitive, possessive, emotional, cautious, caring, a worrier, sentimental, clingy

Leo	The Lion	♌	22 July–23 August	Regulus	Sun	Fire	A natural leader, daring, courageous, likes to be the centre of attention, arrogant, overbearing, self-centred, idealistic, loving, warm-hearted, generous, bossy, intolerant, loyal, image conscious
Virgo	The Virgin	♍	23 August–23 September	Spica	Mercury	Earth	Practical, hard-working, detail orientated, shy, perfectionist, worrier, reliable, meticulous, fussy, conservative
Libra	The Scales	♎	23 September–23 October	Zubeneschamali	Venus	Air	Good listener, charming, sensitive, empathetic, insecure, indecisive, diplomatic
Scorpio	The Scorpion	♏	23 October–22 November	Antares	Mars	Water	Adaptable, strong-willed, passionate, secretive, obstinate, determined, intuitive
Sagittarius	Centaur the Archer	♐	22 November–22 December	Kaus Australis	Jupiter	Fire	Cheerful, sociable, inquisitive, extrovert, frank, carefree and careless, straightforward, honest, tactless, restless

Latin name	English name	Symbol	Dates	Brightest star	Ruled by which planet?	Ruled by which element?	Personality traits
Capricorn	The Goat	♑	22 December– 20 January	Deneb Algedi	Saturn	Earth	Careful, cautious, pessimistic, patient, reserved, prudent, disciplined, practical, reliable, thoughtful, has well-developed sense of humour
Aquarius	The Water Bearer	♒	20 January–18 February	Sadalsuud	Saturn	Air	Idealistic, optimistic, loyal, inventive, unemotional, unpredictable, independent, a dreamer, unconventional, impatient, stubborn, detached
Pisces	The Fishes	♓	18 February– 20 March	Eta Piscium	Jupiter	Water	Thoughtful, compassionate, easily led, weak-willed, escapist, kind, vague, selfless, sympathetic, sensitive, naïve, self-sacrificing, impressionable, impractical, easily distracted

A BRIEF HISTORY OF CHILDBIRTH

AD 98   A Greek doctor named Soranus wrote the first known book on obstetrics, *Gynaecology*. It remained in widespread use up until the sixteenth century.

1500   The earliest documented successful Caesarean was performed by a Swiss pig gelder named Jacob Nufer. After his wife had been in labour for several days, and none of the (thirteen) local midwives had been able to help move things along, he decided to resort to surgery to deliver the baby himself. Both mother and baby survived, and the Nufers went on to have five more children, all delivered naturally.

1540   Publication of *The Byrthe of Mankynde* by Thomas Raynalde, the first book of obstetrics to be printed in English. According to Raynalde,

> The thynges which helpe the byrthe and make it more easie are these. First the woman that laboureth must eyther sytte grovelyng, or else upright, leaning backwarde, according as it shall seeme commodius and necessary to the partie, or as she is accustomed. And in winter or colde weather, the chamber wherein she laboureth must be warmed, but in sommer, or hot weather, let in the ayre to refresh her withal, lest betwene extreme heate and labour the woman faint and fowne. And furthermore, she must be provoked to sneesyng, and that eyther with the powder of Eleborus, or els of Pepper . . .

1591   Eufame Macalyane was burnt alive on Castle Hill in Edinburgh on the order of James I of Scotland (later James VI of England) for daring to ask for pain relief during the birth of her twin sons. Her request was viewed as heretical, since there is a passage in the Bible that is interpreted by some to mean that God intended women to suffer during labour.

1596   The first detailed published account of a Caesarean. It was written by an Italian doctor named Scipione Mercurio. His instructions included the need for four strong assistants to hold the mother down while the incision was made. A liquid concoction of various herbs was then applied, before the baby was removed. There is no record, however, of whether the mother or the baby survived — not a good sign, one would imagine.

On the front page of the 19 November edition of the *Weekly Journal* appeared the story of Mary Toft of Godalming, who was said to have given birth to a rabbit:

> From Guildford comes a strange but well-attested Piece of News. That a poor Woman who lives at Godalmin [sic], near that Town, was about a Month past delivered by Mr John Howard, an Eminent Surgeon and Man-Midwife, of a creature resembling a Rabbit but whose Heart and Lungs grew without its Belly, about 14 Days since she was delivered by the same Person, of a perfect Rabbit: and in a few Days after of 4 more; and on Friday, Saturday, Sunday, the 4th, 5th, and 6th instant, of one in each day: in all nine, they died all in bringing into the World. The woman hath made Oath, that two Months ago, being working in a Field with other Women, they put up a Rabbit, who running from them, they pursued it, but to no Purpose: This created in her such a Longing to it, that she (being with Child) was taken ill and miscarried, and from that Time she hath not been able to avoid thinking of Rabbits.

Despite being embarrassingly verified by Nathaniel St. André, surgeon to George I, Mary Toft's claim was soon revealed to be a hoax. Nonetheless, it reignited debate about the prenatal influence of the imagination, first propounded in Aristotle's *De Generatione et Corruptione* – that is if, while you are pregnant, you are frightened by a rabbit you will give birth to a rabbit or if you eat too much pineapple you will give birth to a baby with a bizarre-shaped head.

1739   William Smellie established Britain's first mid-wifery school in London.

1745   Britain's first lying-in hospital opened in Dublin. Within weeks it was so busy that the mothers had to share beds with each other.

1752   William Smellie's *Treatise on the Theory and Practice of Midwifery*, a classic of its genre, was published. It contained the first instructions on the safe use of forceps, a technique he pioneered.

1774   *The Anatomy of the Gravid Uterus* by William Hunter was published, containing the first detailed anatomical drawings of a pregnant woman.

1793   The first fully verified case of a Caesarean in Britain in which the mother survived. Prior to her pregnancy the patient, Jane Foster of the village of Blackrod near Bolton in Yorkshire, had fallen off a cart and broken her pelvis. Three days into her labour, there was no sign of the baby. Her own doctor refused to attempt a Caesarean, deeming it far too risky, but a Lancashire surgeon named James Barlow agreed to give it a go. The operation took place on Foster's kitchen table, without an anaesthetic; none the less, according to Barlow, 'The poor woman scarcely complained during the operation, so great was her fortitude.' The baby was very sadly stillborn, but Foster made a full recovery.

1817   A rethink of traditional methods of delivering babies was forced by the tragic case of Princess Charlotte, the only child of George IV and the heir to the throne. The princess went into labour two weeks past her due date. It lasted nearly three days, was beset with complications and resulted in a stillborn baby boy. The princess then began to haemorrhage severely, and six hours later she was dead. The public was outraged by the deeply conservative approach that had been taken to her care: why had the obstetrician attending the case, Sir Richard Croft, not tried using forceps? Or even attempted a Caesarean? The debate raged for months, and so widely criticised was Croft that, depressed, he shot himself not long afterwards.

1847   The first use of chloroform to relieve the pain of childbirth. The technique was pioneered by a Scottish doctor named James Young Simpson. Having tested chloroform on himself and been impressed, he decided to try it on the wife of a fellow doctor:

> I placed her under the influence of chloroform, by moistening, with half a tea spoonful of the liquid, a pocket handkerchief, rolled up into a funnel shape, and with the broad or open end of the funnel placed over her mouth and nostrils . . . after the delivery she observed that she had enjoyed a very comfortable sleep . . . but would now be more ready for the work before her . . . it was a matter of no small difficulty to convince the astonished mother that the labour was over and that the child presented to her was really her 'own living baby'.

The mother was so delighted with the outcome that she named her baby daughter Anaesthesia. Suspicions about this new wonder drug lingered, however, until . . .

1853   Chloroform was administered to Queen Victoria to help ease her labour with her eighth child, Leopold. The day after the birth, her doctor Sir James Clark sent a cable to James Young Simpson that read:

> The Queen had chloroform exhibited to her during her late confinement . . . It was not at any time given so strongly as to render the Queen insensible, and an ounce of chloroform was scarcely consumed

during the whole time. Her Majesty was greatly pleased with the effect, and she certainly never has had a better recovery.

Thus pain relief received the royal seal of approval, critics who continued to believe that it was God's will that childbirth was painful were silenced, and chloroform hit the mainstream once and for all.

1880   Louis Pasteur proved that the main cause of puerperal fever (which killed thousands of women, including Henry VIII's third wife Jane Seymour, Mary Wollstonecroft and Mrs. Beeton, who died the day after giving birth to her fourth child) was microbial chains of streptococci. As a result, doctors started to wash their hands regularly between cases for the first time.

1898   German doctor Karl August Bier pioneered the epidural method of pain relief, using a needle to inject cocaine into the lower back of his (male) assistant. To test that the area was indeed numb, Bier 'pulled the man's pubic hair, yanked his testicles, hit him in the legs with a hammer and singed his thighs with a cigar'. Sure enough, his assistant felt no pain. He just had a really bad headache the next day (and a few bruises too, probably).

1902   The Midwives Act made it law that all midwives had to be properly trained and registered.

1929   The College of Obstetricians and Gynaecologists was founded.

1944   The publication of *Childbirth Without Fear* by Grantly Dick-Read, which formed the foundations of the natural birth movement. He argued that pain was a social construct brought on by fear, and that in fact the experience ought just to feel like 'a normal and natural defecation'.

1958   An ultrasound was performed on a pregnant woman for the first time. The technique was pioneered by Professor Ian Donald of Glasgow University, drawing on his knowledge of radar from his time in the R.A.F.

1978   The world's first test-tube (IVF) baby, Louise Brown, was born at Oldham General Hospital in Lancashire.

BABY ANIMALS

THE young of the animal kingdom are mostly called cubs, pups, calves or whelps. Here, however, are a few that aren't.

Alligator	*Hatchling*
Ape	*Infant*
Badger	*Kit*
Beaver	*Kit*
Bee	*Larva*
Cockroach	*Nymph*
Eel	*Elver*
Frog	*Tadpole*
Guinea fowl	*Keet*
Hare	*Leveret*
Hen	*Pullet*
Jellyfish	*Ephyra*
Koala	*Joey*
Llama	*Cria*
Oyster	*Spat*
Partridge	*Cheeper*
Peacock/peafowl	*Peachick*
Platypus	*Puggle*
Spider	*Spiderling*
Turkey	*Poult*

Sweeeeeeeeeeeeeeeet.

THE CASE OF INÉZ RAMÍREZ PÉREZ, THE ONLY WOMAN ON RECORD TO HAVE PERFORMED A SUCCESSFUL SELF-ADMINISTERED CAESAREAN

INÉZ Ramírez Pérez was a forty-year-old peasant woman who lived in a small town in southern Mexico. On the night of 5 March 2000, she went into labour with her eighth child. The nearest clinic was 50 miles away, her husband was out drinking with friends, and she did not have a telephone.

Labour did not progress, and after twelve hours of struggle she became concerned: three years earlier, she had lost a baby during labour, and she was determined not to let this happen again. 'I couldn't stand the pain any more,' she later explained. 'And if my baby was going to die, then I decided I would have to die, too. But if he was going to grow up, I was going to see him grow up, and I was going to be with my child. I thought that God would save both our lives.'

Pérez went to her kitchen and found a 6-inch knife that her husband used to kill animals. She sat down on a low wooden bench under the one-room cabin's single dim electric light and swigged from a bottle of rubbing alcohol. She then made a 17-inch incision in her stomach and, after about an hour, managed to pull the baby out of the uterus. She then cut the umbilical cord with a pair of scissors and promptly fainted. On regaining consciousness, she wrapped a sweater around her stomach to staunch the flow of blood, and then instructed her six-year-old son to go and fetch the village health assistant, who came a few hours later to find Pérez awake and nursing her baby. The health assistant used a regular needle and thread to stitch her up, and then loaded her and the baby on to a straw mat, carried her up a horse track to the town's one paved road and drove for over two and a half hours in a cart over bumpy roads to a clinic.

After receiving basic medical attention, she was then driven eight hours in a pick-up truck to the San Pablo Huixtepec hospital, about 240 miles south of Mexico City, where she was examined by Dr Honorio Galvan and Dr Jesus Guzman. They found that the bleeding had stopped and there was no sign of infection. Four days later, she and her healthy baby boy, whom she named Orlando, were discharged.

Pérez attributed her success in part to her experience in killing animals. There was also an element of luck: because she sat down rather than lay down to perform the operation, she ensured that her uterus was positioned directly underneath her skin, thereby reducing the risk of puncturing her intestines.

The case was verified and reported in the *International Journal of Gynaecology and Obstetrics* in 2004. Both mother and child are still thriving. Pérez has since had her tubes tied.

MOTHERS IN THE BIBLE

Abihail   *Mother of Zuriel, the chief of the Merarite tribe.*

Abijah   *Mother of Hezekiah. Wife of King Ahaz. Daughter of Zechariah.*

Adah (1)   *Mother of Jabal (a shepherd) and Jubal (a musician). First wife of Lamech.*

Adah (2)   *Mother of Eliphaz, the first son of Esau.*

Ahinoam (1)   *Mother of Jonathan, who was a close friend of David. Wife of King Saul.*

Ahinoam (2)   *Mother of David's first son, Amnon. One of David's eight wives.*

Anah   *Mother of Aholibamah, one of Esau's wives.*

Asenath   *Mother of Manasseh and Ephraim. Wife of Joseph.*

Azubah   *Mother of Jehosaphat. Wife of King Asa.*

Bathsheba   *Mother of King Solomon. Wife first of Uriah the Hittite and then of King David.*

Bilhah   *Mother of Dan and Naphtali. She was originally Rachel's handmaid, but Rachel was unable to have children, so she gave Bilhah to her husband, Jacob, as a secondary wife to bear his children.*

Elizabeth   *Mother of John the Baptist. Wife of Zacharias.*

Eve   *Mother of Cain, Abel and Seth. Wife of Adam.*

Hagar   *Mother of Ishmael. She was originally Sarah's handmaid, but Sarah was unable to have children, so she gave Hagar to her husband, Abraham, as a secondary wife to bear his children.*

Haggith   *Mother of Adonijah. Fifth wife of David.*

Hannah   *Mother of the prophet Samuel, followed by three more sons and two daughters. Wife of Elkanah.*

Hephzibah	*Mother of Manasseh. Wife of King Hezekiah.*
Hodiah	*Mother of Jered, Heber and Jeduthiel. Wife of Mered.*
Jedidiah	*Mother of King Josiah. Wife of King Amon.*
Jehoaddan	*Mother of King Amaziah. Wife of King Jehoash.*
Jerusha	*Mother of King Jotham. Wife of King Uzziah.*
Jochebed	*Mother of the prophet Moses, as well as of Aaron and Miriam. Wife of Amram.*
Keturah	*Mother of six sons (Zimran, Jokshan, Medan, Midian, Isbak and Shuah), each of whom fathered one of the six tribes of Palestine. Abraham's third wife after the death of Sarah.*
Leah	*Mother of six sons (Reuben, Simeon, Levi, Judah, Issachar and Zebulan) and one daughter (Dinah). First wife of Jacob, even though Jacob was in love with her sister, Rachel.*
Maachah (1)	*Mother of Peresh and Sheresh.*
Maachah (2)	*Mother of Absolom. One of David's eight wives.*
Maachah (3)	*Mother of King Abijah.*
Mary	*Mother of Jesus. Wife of Joseph.*
Matred	*Mother of Mehetabel.*
Merab	*Mother of five sons, all of whom were hanged by the Gibeonites as revenge against her father, Saul.*
Meshullemeth	*Mother of Amon. Wife of Manaseh.*
Naamah	*Mother of Rehoboam. One of Solomon's many wives.*
Naomi	*Mother of Mahlon and Chilion. Husband of Elimelech. Mother-in-law of Ruth.*
Nehushta	*Mother of King Jehoiachin. Wife of King Jehoiakim.*
Rachel	*Mother of Joseph and Benjamin. Wife of Jacob.*
Rahab	*Mother of Boaz. Wife of Salmon.*

Rebekah	Mother of Jacob and Esau. Wife of Isaac.
Reumah	Mother of Tebah, Gaham, Thahash and Maachah. Secondary wife of Nahor. The first woman in the Bible to be described as a concubine.
Rizpah	Mother of four sons, including Armoni, Megphibosheth and Ishbosheth. One of Saul's concubines.
Ruth	Mother of Obed. Wife of Boaz.
Salome	Mother of James and John. Wife of Zebedee.
Sarah	Mother of Isaac, whom she bore to her husband, Abraham, when she was over a hundred years old. Many did not believe this and accused her of having adopted a foundling. To prove them wrong, Abraham invited everyone over for a banquet on the day Isaac was due to be weaned. Sarah offered up her own breast milk to all the guests' babies, which succeeded in convincing them that a miracle had occurred.

THE BRITISH ROYAL FAMILY

Name	Date of birth	Time of birth	Place of birth
The Queen	21 April 1926	2.40 a.m.	17 Bruton Place, London W1
The Duke of Edinburgh	10 June 1921	Not known	Villa Mon Repos, Corfu
The Prince of Wales	14 November 1948	9.14 p.m.	Buckingham Palace*
The Duchess of Cornwall	17 July 1947	Not known	King's College Hospital, London

* The first royal birth since that of James II in 1633 *not* to be witnessed by a representative of the people (who in later years was always the Home Secretary) to ensure that the baby was not a changeling.

Name	Date of birth	Time of birth	Place of birth
Prince William	21 June 1982	9.03 p.m.	St Mary's Hospital, Paddington, London
Prince Harry	15 September 1984	4.20 p.m.	St Mary's Hospital, Paddington, London
The Duke of York	19 February 1960	3.30 p.m.	Buckingham Palace*
Princess Beatrice	8 August 1988	8.18 p.m.	Portland Hospital, London
Princess Eugenie	23 March 1990	7.58 p.m.	Portland Hospital, London†
The Earl of Wessex	10 March 1964	8.20 p.m.	Buckingham Palace
The Countess of Wessex	20 January 1965	Not known	Radcliffe Infirmary, Oxford
James, Viscount Severn	17 December 2007	4.20 p.m.	Frimley Park Hospital, Surrey
Lady Louise Windsor	8 November 2003	11.32 p.m.	Frimley Park Hospital, Surrey§
The Princess Royal	15 August 1950	11.50 a.m.	Clarence House
Peter Phillips	15 November 1977	10.46 a.m.	St Mary's Hospital, Paddington, London**
Zara Phillips	15 May 1981	8.15 p.m.	St Mary's Hospital, Paddington, London

---

* The palace's Belgian suite, to be precise.
† The first royal baby to have a public christening.
§ Born a few weeks' premature by emergency Caesarean section, necessitated by a placental abruption.
** The first royal baby to be born without any title – that is, to be born a commoner – since the children of Cecily of York, the daughter of Edward IV, in the 1480s. The reason for this was that Princess Anne possesses no hereditary title herself, and is said to have rejected an offer from the Queen to allow the baby to be born into the peerage.

MONTH TO MONTH

IN 1870, Tiffany & Co. (who obviously had a vested interest in the matter) published a pamphlet with the following verses, which formalized the traditional association of stone with a month. It is to be noted that the anonymous author was not particularly original or indeed industrious in his attempt at poetry: the repetition of the verses for January, March and June would suggest he or she could have tried a little harder . . .

By her who in January was born
No gem save garnets shall be worn
They will ensure her constancy
True friendship and fidelity.

The February born shall find
Sincerity and peace of mind,
Freedom from passion and from care,
If they, the amethyst will wear.

By her who in March was born
No gem save bloodstone shall be worn
They will ensure her constancy
True friendship and fidelity.

She who from April dates her years,
Diamonds shall wear,
Lest bitter tears
For vain repentance flow.

Who first beholds the light of day
In spring's sweet, flower month of May
And wears an emerald all her life
Shall be a loved and a loving wife.

By her who in June was born
No gem save pearls shall be worn
They will ensure her constancy
True friendship and fidelity.

The gleaming ruby should adorn,
All those who in July are born,
For thus they'll be exempt and free,
From lover's doubts and anxiety.

Wear a peridot or for thee,
No conjugal fidelity,
The August born without this stone,
'Tis said, must live unloved; alone.

A maiden born when autumn leaves
Are rustling in September's breeze,
A sapphire on her brow should bind;
To bring her joy and peace of mind.

October's child is born for woe,
And life's vicissitudes must know,
But lay an opal on her breast,
And hope will lull those woes to rest.

Who first comes to this world below
In dreary November's fog and snow,
Should prize the topaz amber hue,
Emblem of friends and lovers true.

If cold December gave you birth
The month of snow and ice and mirth
Place on your hand a turquoise blue;
Success will bless whate'er you do

36.5 PER CENT OF WOMEN HAVE AN EPIDURAL, AND VARIOUS OTHER STATISTICS SURROUNDING THE GREAT MYSTERY THAT IS CHILDBIRTH

WHETHER you give birth alone like the freebirthers or silently like Scientologists, or anywhere else in between, the fact is that as long as baby and mum are OK, who cares? The rest is just detail. Well, as long as you don't give birth to, say, an elephant, as Alcippe did, according to Pliny's *Natural History* of c.AD 77–9. Humans are the only mammal species who regularly need help giving birth: the reason for this is that our pelvises are extremely narrow compared to those of other primates, in order to allow us to walk upright. It also does not help that the heads of newborn human babies are proportionally so enormous, measuring about 6 per cent of the mother's weight compared to 2 per cent in the case of a gorilla's offspring. No wonder, then, that a fair proportion of British mothers needed a bit of intervention . . .

	Total deliveries	Spontaneous		Forceps		Ventouse
		Vertex	Other	Low	Other	
1980	601,500	75.5	1.0	6.2	5.1	0.7
1982	574,600	75.8	1.1	5.7	4.6	0.6
1983	578,400	75.3	2.1	5.6	4.2	0.6
1984	586,100	75.8	2.0	5.5	4.2	0.6
1985	605,100	75.4	2.5	5.3	3.8	0.7
1989–90	633,500	76.7	1.4	3.9	3.9	1.6
1990–91	652,100	75.6	1.1	4.0	3.5	2.1
1991–2	643,800	75.1	1.2	3.9	3.0	2.7
1992–3	624,600	74.4	1.1	3.6	3.0	3.1
1993–4	620,200	72.5	1.3	3.5	3.0	3.7
1994–5	604,300	71.5	1.3	3.3	2.5	4.8
1995–6	592,600	70.8	1.5	2.8	2.3	5.4
1996–7	594,500	70.6	1.1	2.4	2.1	5.9
1997–8	585,000	69.2	1.0	2.2	1.7	6.5
1998–9	577,500	67.7	1.2	2.0	1.7	7.1
1999–2000	565,300	66.3	1.1	2.0	1.8	7.4
2000–1	549,600	65.1	1.5	2.1	1.7	7.2
2001–2	541,700	65.6	0.9	2.0	1.5	7.2
2002–3	548,000	65.9	1.0	1.9	1.5	7.1
2003–4	575,900	65.5	1.0	1.7	1.6	7.0
2004–5	584,100	65.0	0.8	2.8	1.7	7.2
2005–6	593,400	64.2	0.7	2.0	1.9	7.2
2005–6 (new methodology)	611,337	64.0	0.4	2.0	2.0	7.1
2006–7	629,207	63.5	0.4	2.2	2.3	7.0
2007–8	649,837	62.5	0.4	2.2	2.8	7.0
2008–9	652,638	62.4	0.5	2.3	3.2	6.6

Breech	Breech extraction	Caesarean		Total*	Other	Unknown method of delivery†
		Elective	Other/ emergency			
1.2	1.3	4.0	5.0	9.0	0.1	
1.0	1.0	4.6	5.5	10.1	0.0	
0.9	1.0	4.6	5.5	10.1	0.1	
0.9	0.9	4.6.	5.5	10.1	0.1	
0.9	0.9	4.9	5.5	10.4	0.1	
0.8	0.3	4.9	6.3	11.3	0.2	
0.8	0.3	5.3	7.1	12.4	0.1	
0.8	0.2	5.5	7.4	12.9	0.2	
0.7	0.2	5.6	8.1	13.8	0.2	
0.7	0.2	6.1	8.9	15.0	0.2	
0.7	0.2	6.5	9.0	15.5	0.2	
0.7	0.2	6.9	9.5	16.3	0.1	
0.7	0.1	7.3	9.7	17.0	0.3	
0.5	0.1	7.9	10.4	18.2	0.5	
0.5	0.1	8.0	11.1	19.1	0.6	
0.4	0.1	8.6	12.0	20.6	0.4	
0.5	0.1	8.8	12.7	21.5	0.4	
0.3	0.1	9.3	12.7	22.0	0.3	
0.3	0.1	9.3	12.7	22.0	0.2	
0.3	0.1	9.6	13.1	22.7	0.2	
0.3	0.1	9.4	13.6	22.9	0.2	
0.3	0.1	9.3	14.1	23.5	0.2	
0.4	0.0	9.5	14.6	24.1	0.0	36,322
0.4	0.0	9.5	14.7	24.3	0.0	31,176
0.4	0.1	9.7	14.9	24.6	0.0	26,324
0.4	0.1	9.8	14.8	24.6	0.0	22,999

Source: NHS Information Centre

---

* Percentages may not add up because of rounding of decimal places.
† The numbers of unknowns were not published prior to 2006–7.

652,638 babies born in a hospital in 2008–9?* That works out as 1,788 babies born a day or 1.24 babies a minute, which is a pretty astonishing thought. Alongside these statistics exist a veritable plethora of other, equally fascinating ones about childbirth in the UK in the twenty-first century. For instance: of those women who had a spontaneous delivery, 36.5 per cent had an epidural, general or spinal anaesthetic during labour; 8.3 per cent had an episiotomy; 12.2 per cent were instrumental deliveries; 74 per cent spent a day or less in hospital afterwards. Of the 24.6 per cent of births that were by Caesarean section, the highest rate was at Chelsea and Westminster Hospital, London (33.3 per cent) and the lowest rate was at Sherwood Forest Hospital, Nottinghamshire (15.8 per cent). This is all in addition, of course, to the little less than 3 per cent of babies who were born at home.†

UNITED NATIONS CONVENTION ON THE RIGHTS OF THE CHILD

THE United Nations Convention on the Rights of the Child covers everything from the need for every baby to have a name to the importance of access to clean drinking water to the right to play. It came into force in 1990, and has been ratified by every country in the world except Somalia and the USA. Here are the first eight articles (out of a total of fifty-four).

---

* The first tour of the hospital is terrifying. Do not go with a pregnant friend, because you will just egg each other on in the realms of terror.

† Home births are the most likely place to encounter placenta eating (technically known as placentophagia), which is said to replace vital vitamins and minerals lost in the birth process. *Placenta* is, after all, the Latin word for 'cake'. Popular recipes include lasagne or Bolognese.

Article 1

For the purposes of the present Convention, a child means every human being below the age of eighteen years unless under the law applicable to the child, majority is attained earlier.

Article 2

1. States Parties shall respect and ensure the rights set forth in the present Convention to each child within their jurisdiction without discrimination of any kind, irrespective of the child's or his or her parent's or legal guardian's race, colour, sex, language, religion, political or other opinion, national, ethnic or social origin, property, disability, birth or other status.

2. States Parties shall take all appropriate measures to ensure that the child is protected against all forms of discrimination or punishment on the basis of the status, activities, expressed opinions, or beliefs of the child's parents, legal guardians, or family members.

Article 3

1. In all actions concerning children, whether undertaken by public or private social welfare institutions, courts of law, administrative authorities or legislative bodies, the best interests of the child shall be a primary consideration.

2. States Parties undertake to ensure the child such protection and care as is necessary for his or her well-being, taking into account the rights and duties of his or her parents, legal guardians, or other individuals legally responsible for him or her, and, to this end, shall take all appropriate legislative and administrative measures.

3. States Parties shall ensure that the institutions, services and facilities responsible for the care or protection of children shall conform with the standards established by competent authorities, particularly in the areas of safety, health, in the number and suitability of their staff, as well as competent supervision.

Article 4

States Parties shall undertake all appropriate legislative, administrative, and other measures for the implementation of the rights recognized in the present Convention. With regard to economic, social and cultural rights, States Parties shall undertake such measures to the maximum extent of their available resources and, where needed, within the framework of international co-operation.

Article 5

States Parties shall respect the responsibilities, rights and duties of parents or, where applicable, the members of the extended family or community as provided for by local custom, legal guardians or other persons legally responsible for the child, to provide, in a manner consistent with the evolving capacities of the child, appropriate direction and guidance in the exercise by the child of the rights recognized in the present Convention.

Article 6

1. States Parties recognize that every child has the inherent right to life.
2. States Parties shall ensure to the maximum extent possible the survival and development of the child.

Article 7

1. The child shall be registered immediately after birth and shall have the right from birth to a name, the right to acquire a nationality and, as far as possible, the right to know and be cared for by his or her parents.
2. States Parties shall ensure the implementation of these rights in accordance with their national law and their obligations under the relevant international instruments in this field, in particular where the child would otherwise be stateless.

Article 8

1. States Parties undertake to respect the right of the child to preserve his or her identity, including nationality, name and family relations as recognized by law without unlawful interference.

2. Where a child is illegally deprived of some or all of the elements of his or her identity, States Parties shall provide appropriate assistance and protection, with a view to re-establishing speedily his or her identity.

Source: United Nations

A FEW EXCLAMATIONS TO SHOUT OUT DURING LABOUR; OR, HOW TO AVOID SHOCKING THE MIDWIFE

Blast

Botheration

Bums

Crikey

Damn

Damnation

Drat

Fiddlesticks

Fudge

Holy bananas

Holy mackerel

Holy moly

Jeepers creepers

Jeez Louise

Jiminy Cricket

Leaping lizards

Oy vey

Shoot

Sugar

Sugar-plum fairies

WORLD RECORDS

Most children born to one woman: 69. Russian peasant Feodor Vassilyev was pregnant 27 times between 1725 and 1765, giving birth to 16 sets of twins, 7 sets of triplets and 4 sets of quadruplets.

Shortest interval between two births: 208 days. Jayne Bleackley of New Zealand gave birth to a son on 3 September 1999, and then a daughter on 30 March 2000.

Longest interval between two births: 41 years and 185 days. Elizabeth Ann Buttle of Wales gave birth to a daughter in 1956, and then a son in 1997 at the age of 60.

Oldest mother to give birth to a baby who was conceived naturally: Dawn Brooke of Guernsey. In 1997 she gave birth to a son at the age of 59.

Oldest woman to give birth to a baby who was conceived by IVF: Maria del Carmen Bousada Lara of Spain. In 2006, she gave birth to twin boys at the age of 66 years and 358 days.

Youngest mother: Lina Medina of Peru. In 1939 she gave birth to a 6-pound baby boy at the age of 5 years, 7 months and 21 days.

Most premature baby who survived: Amillia Sonja Taylor. She was born at 21 weeks and 6 days, weighing just under 10 ounces, in Miami in 2006.

Most surviving babies from a single birth: 8. Nadja Suleman gave birth to octuplets in Bellflower, California, in 2009. She named them Noah, Maliyah, Isaiah, Nariyah, Jonah, Jeremiah, Makai and Josiah.

THE FIRST COUPLE OF DAYS FOLLOWING THE BIRTH OF THE FUTURE GEORGE IV ON 12 AUGUST 1762, AT ST JAMES'S PALACE, IN THE WORDS OF THE ATTENDING DOCTOR

Soon after [the birth of the Prince] we examined him all over, and found him perfect, with every mark of health, and of a large size. Then we examined the placenta which was sound and very compleat, and Mrs Draper told us that the Queen had had a very good time, and was very well.

A little after 9, when her Majesty had shifted, we saw what was taken from the bed, and found it just moderate or what is most common: then I saw the Queen (who had taken a little N. meg and Sugar after delivery) and found her without any complaint and with a good pulse. We ordered for Her Majesty:

R – Spt. Cit. Sol. ʒi
Pulv. Contr. C. ʒiss

Aq. Alex. Simp. f℥iss

− N. M. f℥iss

Syr. Croc. f℥ss

M ft Haustus

6ta quaque hora sum*

and for the Prince

R − Ol. Amygd. D. ℨii

Syr. Ros. ℨvi

Rhubarb gr. iii. M.

Cap. Cochl parvum omni hora[†]

At 12 o'clock we saw the Q. again and found her perfectly well, and her pulse more quiet than when we left her in the morning.

She had taken some broth and one draught, and had had a

---

* This Latin prescription for the mother translates as:

Spirits of Lemon 1 scruple [believed to relieve nausea]
Compounded powder of Contrayerva 1½ scruples [made from the root of the Dorstenia plant and a gentle stimulant]
Alexiterial Water 1½ fluid ounces [water mixed with sea wormwood tops, angelica leaves and spearmint leaves]
Nutmeg 1½ fluid drams [an astringent, also thought to help with diarrhoea]
Syrup of saffron ½ fluid dram [believed to help cleanse a woman's uterus]
Mix to make draught
To be taken ever six hours

† This Latin prescription for the baby translates as:

Sweet Almonds oil, 2 drams [for colic − often given to a baby as soon as it was born]
Syrup of Damask Roses, 6 drams [a mild purgative]
Rhubarb, 3 grains [also a mild purgative]
A small spoonful every hour

refreshing sleep. She desired to live some days upon broth, caudle and tea, rather than to eat chicken.

The Prince had taken the 2nd large Tea Spoonful of the purging mixture, was quiet and looked extremely well.

At 6 in the evening the Q. had slept an hour and was remarkably well. She had eaten with appetite – had made water plentifully and with ease – the clothes were of a full colour and in plenty. She now took her 2nd Hausrus and was ordered a Spoonful of Wine in each half pint of caudle.

At this time the Prince had his first stool and made water but had not sucked.

At 10 at night we were informed that the Q. was well, and therefore did not go in. We gave orders that, if any considerable rigor should come on within 36 hours from delivery, to give immediately a small glass of Brandy and to send for me.

The Prince was quite well, had had another stool, and had sucked several times.

Friday, 13 August 1762. At ½ after 10 we visited the Prince. He looked well, had sucked and slept comfortably through the night, and had 3 or 4 stools. Order: to let the Beast [sic] be his principal support, but to feed him twice a day, as had been the custom in the Princess of Wales' family. The Princess desired a little milk to be put into the Pap.

The Queen had rested well, particularly had one continued sleep from midnight to four o'clock; her pulse remarkably quick, yet not slow. She was cheerful and said she had no complaint; cleansed well and still of deep or full colour, and made water easily; had not desire to eat chicken: thought the draught made her thirsty, therefore I wrote thus:

R –   Spt. Cit. Sol. ℈i
        Pulv. Contr. Co. ℈iss

Aq. Ros. fȝiss

– N. M. fȝiss

Syr. Ros. ȝsss

Ft haust 6ta quaque h. Sum

Her Majesty asked if she might see the Prince. We allowed it with proper caution and gave Direction to Mrs Scott.

At 7 in the evening. The Prince perfectly well.

The Q. had taken plenty of Berry or caudle (which she liked better than broth), and bread and Butter with Tea, had slept ½ hour twice – was in cheerful spirits and fine perspiration.

William Hunter, *An Obstetric Diary of 1762–5*

HOW TO TAKE A PHOTO OF A NEWBORN BABY

BABY photos are an eminently tricky proposition, given the generally unco-operative nature of the subject matter. Add to this the problem of a newborn's strange physical quirks (weird skin issues, an odd-shaped head, the expression of a drunk old man and so on) and it really becomes imperative to know all the tricks. So . . .

– Pick the moment carefully: directly after a feed is ideal, as is naptime – most babies tend to be rather more compliant when they are actually asleep.

– Ensure the background is plain, without anything extraneous that might distract the viewer's attention from the little cherub.

- Whenever possible, use natural light. Make sure it is a shaded area, though, rather than direct sunlight. A cloudy day is perfect. If there is no choice but to be indoors, try increasing the camera's ISO setting as well as the aperture setting in order to keep flash to a minimum, not least for the baby's sake (unless he is a celebrity baby, of course, in which case he needs to be trained for the paparazzi from the earliest possible age).
- Get down to the baby's level. If necessary, lie on the ground.
- Close-ups always work well. Ideally, though, use a long focal lens instead of continually shoving the camera in the baby's face.
- Find a way to give some sense of proportion in the photo – that is, of how very tiny the baby's hand/foot/nose is compared to the rest of the world. Also take some photos of these appendages alone, to make a change from just 'another day, another outfit'.
- Make use of the camera's burst mode (also called contin-uous mode) to take lots of shots in quick succession, and hence increase the chances of hitting upon the one perfect one.
- Always keep the camera handy. Consider buying more than one camera, even a few disposables, to have in each room.
- All photos look more elegant in black and white. It also helps smooth out any blemishes, thereby avoiding having to resort to Photoshopping the baby. Who are you, Anna Wintour?

WILLIAM BLAKE ON BABIES

Infant Joy (first published in 1789)

'I have no name;
I am but two days old.'
What shall I call thee?
'I happy am,
Joy is my name.'
Sweet joy befall thee!

Pretty joy!
Sweet joy, but two days old.
Sweet Joy I call thee:
Thou dost smile,
I sing the while;
Sweet joy befall thee!

Infant Sorrow (first published in 1794)

My mother groan'd! my father wept.
Into the dangerous world I leapt.
Helpless, naked, piping loud;
Like a fiend hid in a cloud.

Struggling in my father's hands,
Striving against my swaddling bands;
Bound and weary I thought best
To sulk upon my mother's breast.

SLEEPING: SOME STATISTICS

ALLOWING BABY TO SLEEP IN THE PARENTAL BED

How often	Percentage of babies
All the time	4 per cent
Regularly	7 per cent
Sometimes	15 per cent
Rarely	23 per cent
Never	51 per cent

PLACING OF BABY TO SLEEP

Position of baby	Percentage of babies
On baby's back	84 per cent
On baby's front	2 per cent
On baby's side	6 per cent
Varies	7 per cent
Not stated	1 per cent

Source: NHS Infant Feeding Survey, 2007

THE FIRST WEEK

'I AM told that only one person, Zoroaster, laughed on the day he was born, and that his fontanelle pulsated so much that it dislodged hands placed on his head, which was an omen of future knowledge,' wrote Pliny in his *Natural History*. This just goes to show that newborns are full of surprises; there is simply no way of predicting how s/he will behave. And no wonder. The trouble with babies is that, inconveniently, every single one is different. They are people first and babies second. Nobody assumes that you and I both need exactly the same amount of sleep as Michelle Obama, so it is a mystery why childcare experts apply these bonkers rules to babies. The primary goals in these early days are 1. to keep the baby alive and 2. to get to know him (or her). After all, you have essentially only just met. You hardly know each other. The relationship is in its very earliest stages, and communication problems abound. It takes time to become familiar with each other's needs and wants and what each cry means (him: I need a nap, you: I need a nap), what each arch of the back means (him: I'm bored and I'd like to go for a walk please, you: I'm stir-crazy and I'd like to go for a walk, so 'fuckity bye'* to the lot of you).

Throughout these early days, cling on to the fact that the first hundred days of this strange new job of yours are, in most cases, by far the hardest (for some women, they are the hardest of their entire life) and thereafter it does get a lot easier. Promise. Cling to the fact that this bewildering existence is not now your new life for ever – though it might feel like for ever

---

*　With thanks to Malcolm Tucker

at the time – but rather a very temporary aberration that zips by so fast that cases have been documented of nostalgia setting in before it is even over.

At this stage, most of the babycare manuals one has likely pored over during the previous nine months suddenly reveal themselves to be all but irrelevant. The baby is still adjusting to this too bright, too noisy world of ours, and hence for the first couple of weeks or so one has pretty much zero control over the baby's sleep cycle: s/he will fall asleep anytime, any place, anywhere, and there is very little you can do about it. Do not fight it, which will just result in frustration all round; instead, shamble through as best you can and try to enjoy being free from the tyranny of babycare manuals, for a short while at least.

If anyone asks you what they can do to help, ask them please to place (and pay for) an online supermarket order for you. Ready meals, fresh fruit, overpriced smoothies: anything, really, to keep the new mother fed and nourished (in particular, the breastfeeding new mother, out of whom all the vitamins and minerals are being sucked by the little vampire). Your mother or mother-in-law ought to come and stay only if you are entirely confident that they will really and truly help: that is, that they will ungrudgingly a) cook, b) clean and c) give advice only when directly asked for it. Otherwise, politely suggest she stay away in the very early days, and instead revel with your partner in the cocoon of your newly expanded family, both of you awake at 3.00 a.m. earnestly debating whether changing a poo-filled nappy is worth risking the baby waking up in the process, and other such complex issues.

When visitors come round (invite only those who you are absolutely certain will be happy to make their own tea and bring their own biscuits; otherwise they are not welcome), do not expect too much of them. Not all of us know how to coo over a baby; we were simply not taught it at school. Take Fanny in Nancy Mitford's *The Pursuit of Love* when she goes to visit her cousin Linda just after she has given birth:

> ... deep down among the frills and lace, there was the usual horrid sight of a howling orange in a fine black wig.
>
> 'Isn't she sweet,' said the Sister. 'Look at her little hands.'
>
> I shuddered slightly, and said:
>
> 'Well, I know it's dreadful of me, but I don't much like them as small as that; I'm sure she'll be divine in a year or two.'
>
> The wails now entered a crescendo, and the whole room was filled with hideous noise.
>
> 'Poor soul,' said Linda. 'I think it must have caught sight of itself in a glass. Do take it away, Sister.'

Angelina Jolie was viciously vilified for describing her newborn babies as 'blobs', but let's be honest, she had a point. There will be much discussion in the first few days about whom the baby looks like. This is a total waste of time, because the fact is that every newborn looks like his or her father. It is nature's way of making sure he knows the baby is his to take care of. So anyone who says the baby looks like the mother is just flattering her – not that there is anything wrong with a bit of flattery, of course, especially when one is lying around in one's pyjamas having not shaved one's legs for a fortnight. In fact, at this stage it is more advisable for guests to pass comment on the mother than on the baby. Here is what she wants to hear: 'You are doing brilliantly and it's quite obvious already that you're a fantastic mother and also, incidentally, a fabulously beautiful one.' Someone, anyone, please?

CAFFEINE

CAFFEINE is a chemical compound consisting of carbon, hydrogen, nitrogen and oxygen – or, $C_8H_{10}N_4O_2$.

As a new mother, one tends to spend an unhealthy amount of time thinking about this wonder drug: how soon am I allowed yet another a cup of tea? Is it wrong of me to leave my baby to cry for a mo whilst I nip to the kitchen to make one? All the while hoping that by some miracle s/he might even have stopped crying by the time I return? How do I avoid spilling said cup of tea down said baby, who wants to be held all the time? Or indeed, said mother? And so on.

	Type of drink	Caffeine content in milligrams
Tea	A 6oz cup brewed for 1 minute	10–40
	A 6oz cup brewed for 3 minutes	20–55
	A 6oz cup brewed for 5 minutes	25–100
Coffee	A 6oz cup of drip coffee	130–180
	A 6oz cup of percolated coffee	75–150
	A 6oz cup of instant coffee	50–130
	A 6oz cup of decaffeinated coffee	2–6
Chocolate	Milk chocolate (1oz)	6
	Dark chocolate (1oz)	20
	M&Ms (1.75oz, i.e. a packet)	15
Other	A 12oz can of Coca-Cola	46
	A 12oz can of Diet Coca-Cola	46

The conclusion? After a really sleepless night, nip out to a garage and inject yourself with some good old-fashioned drip coffee. The outing will cheer you up, too, if only by allowing you to browse the racks of celebrity magazines screaming 'BACK TO THE CATWALK TWO WEEKS POST-BABY!!!' Oh no, hang on a minute: it will just depress you even more. Oh well.

CARS

THE arrival of a newborn was once the death knell for fun in car purchasing. A typical seventies sitcom 'B' plot would involve the male of the house selling his beloved MG/Triumph Spitfire two-seater sports car and grudgingly agreeing to buy, at the behest of his wife, the dull Austin Princess or Rover 2000 – a 'sensible family man's' car. The underlying message being of course, 'Your life is over.' From now on it's driving gloves and golf. And then death.

Luckily for the driver at the beginning of the twenty-first century, this is no longer the case. Sure, you can't really fit a baby seat in the back of most sports cars (well, you can in both the Porsche 911 and Jaguar XK, but expect a few hostile looks from other mothers), but the range of cars available to choose from is exponentially greater.

For a start, nearly all today's cars are far bigger, both inside and out, than the cars of twenty or thirty years ago. This means that you can fit a car seat (for those with just the one child) in nearly any car, even the new Fiat 500 – I've seen it done. It is no longer instantly necessary to rush out and buy an estate car, since most cars these days have very sizeable boots which, given that buggies and prams are increasingly foldable and light-weight, means they will do a very good job on a day-to-day basis. So if size is no longer that important as a variable, what should be considered?

Obviously the first issue is fuel economy. Actually, that is the second thing. The first thing is 'Do I look cool in this car?' Or, to put it another way, 'Would I buy this car anyway — *even if I didn't have a child?*' Ideally with the car of choice you should answer yes to both questions. Hybrids are an obvious starting point. The Toyota Prius is a popular (if dull) choice. It looks OK, is well equipped and delivers good fuel economy and very low CO_2 output. But since a Prius is available only as a hybrid, it does rather shout one's green credentials, when hybrid models by other manufacturers are just the hybrid version of another model: for example, the Honda Civic Hybrid looks exactly like the normal Honda Civic. So a lot more subtle.

Another option, of course, is to go diesel. Often offering better fuel economy than hybrids, diesel engines are let down only by relatively higher CO_2 emissions, and those are improving enormously. The Ford Fiesta Econetic is an excellent choice: it gets 78 miles to the gallon and emissions of just 98g/km. The Seat Ibiza Ecomotive (notice car manufacturers' clever use of 'eco' in just about everything) offers similar performance of 76 miles to the gallon and 99g/km.

However, if you are the proud parents of two or more offspring, you will need more space, bearing in mind that the amount of 'stuff' you accumulate is exponentially related to the number of children you have:

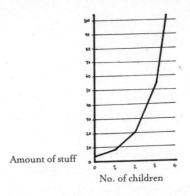

Amount of stuff

No. of children

Furthermore, just as cars have got bigger so it would seem that car seats have grown with them. Sitting between two car seats is a challenge in most small to medium-sized cars these days. So once the second child arrives, it is time (assuming you think there will sometimes be a need for either a parent or a friend to travel in the back with them, for whatever reason) to start looking for bigger cars.

The good news is that big cars these days can also, shockingly, still be cool and economical. The Skoda Yeti, for example. OK, it is not exactly cool, but it is economical (44mpg, 149 g/km CO_2) and was *Top Gear*'s Family Car of the Year last year. And those terrible *Top Gear* men know what they are talking about when it comes to one thing (and one thing only): motor cars. For those with a bit more spending power, there is the private-school-car-park-ubiquitous 'luxury green' of the Lexus RX450h. However, for those who want to have a bit more fun, consider this: these days, it really is relatively easy to pick up a ten-year-old second-hand Range Rover for under £10K and either convert it to LPG or have the diesel retrofitted to be able to use biodiesel. It is the car that Prince Charles drives. So: size, fabulousness, price, green credentials *and* by royal appointment, all in one handy package. Ding dong.

JOHN LOCKE

EVEN the greatest minds have not always got it right when it comes to babies. Sure, John Locke invented the idea that a newborn is a blank slate, a *tabula rasa*, formed entirely by experience – that is, nurture – rather than nature (aargh, the pressure!). But in a diary entry in 1684 about how to care for a newborn, he advocated holding a steak to its bottom to give it strength, so what did he know? I dare you to try to explain that one to the health visitor.

1. Soon after birth the baby can be given 1 or 2 spoonfuls of syrup of violets with almond oil, to loosen the bowels and keep it from convulsive colic. Or else distilled olive oil can be mixed with sugar.

2. If the newborn baby is in a weak condition you can blow on it the smell of chewed onions and cloves; smear its nostrils and lips with Cinnamon water; press warm slices of meat on its head and anus; wrap in bandages soaked in red wine and place in a bath composed of water or beer and fresh butter. If the baby is lively give a little after a mixture of 1 spoonful of distilled almond oil and syrup of Cowslip flowers and spoonful of wine tempered with sugar, so that it can purge itself properly.

3. As soon as it begins to feed on pap, give it for the first few days a little powder of Marchion.

4. If it is weak apply to the region of the heart a cloth coated with warm Embryon. The best ways to stimulate its strength are baths, putting warm wine on its head, placing hot meat on its chest, smearing its nose and lips with cinnamon water, putting onions near its nostrils, etc.

YOU, THE PANTHER

THERE are few noises in life more dispiriting than the creaking of an unfortunate floorboard on the threshold of your baby's boudoir as you inexpertly walk out of the room, having finally persuaded your stubborn baby that the Land of Nod is indeed worth a visit for the night. So follow these simple tricks to ensure such a situation does not arise.

First, address the matter of your feet. Shoes are obviously too noisy, even soft-soled ones, while the trace of moisture that is always on bare feet means they too disturb the peace as they peel away from the floor each time you take a step. Socks, then, are what are called for.

Next, carefully consider the choice of clothing for the task at hand. The ideal attire is no attire – that is, naked. Failing that, silk pyjamas are the next best thing. If for some strange reason neither of these are an option, at least wear clothes made of a soft fabric such as wool, rather than, say, denim, which when rubbed together by the movement of the legs can be jolly noisy. Be sure your outfit is either tight or well tucked in, so as not to risk random bits of fabric billowing about. Also be wary of jewellery such as dangly necklaces or jangly bracelets.

With these preparations complete, the next challenge is to perfect the way you walk. Walking on tiptoes as though you are in a cartoon is a possibility, but the trouble is that this approach puts you at serious risk of losing your balance. So instead, try placing the heel on the ground first and then slowly rolling the rest of the foot forward until the ball of the foot is also on the ground. The toes should stay raised at all times. Do not shift your weight from one foot to another until the foot is firmly on the ground, and keep as much of the weight as possible on the outer edge of the foot.

With each step, minimize the creaking of the floorboards by walking as close to the wall as possible, where the floor is better supported. Similarly on stairs, stick to the very edge, ideally on the wall side, staying well away from the centre of each step, which is where the creak will be the loudest. Consider taking two or three steps at a time, but again beware of losing your balance. If it is possible to avoid floorboards altogether and just stick to carpeted areas, so much the better.

Bearing in mind that the speed of sound is about 1,120 feet (about 340 metres) a second, try to capitalize on any sort of noise that the baby might seem about to make — rolling over, coughing, that sort of thing — by taking a step a fraction of a second beforehand. The slight delay should then mask any slight noise that you yourself mistakenly make.

Once you reach your destination — the sofa in front of the telly, one assumes, enormous glass of wine a-waiting — remember to breathe, smile and enjoy the peace, in the full knowledge that you are not alone in the complicated feelings you will often experience at this point: one of the great paradoxes about babies is that the minute they are asleep, you are desperate for them to wake up, but the minute they wake up, you are desperate for them to go to sleep. We parents are strange creatures indeed.

FLIPPING OUT; OR, SIX COMMON BUT WEIRD WAYS IN WHICH ONE'S BODY CHANGES POSTPARTUM THAT NOBODY EVER WARNS ONE ABOUT

1. Hair loss. Often in huge clumps.
2. Sudden increase in dental cavities.
3. Excessive sweating.
4. Stiff, numb and/or painful joints (a bit like arthritis or carpel tunnel syndrome).
5. Haemorrhoids, anal fissures and incontinence, even after a Caesarean, and all sorts of other unmentionables that one would rather not think about.
6. A general but permanent shift in body chemistry, resulting in a variety of symptoms including an increase in warts, intensified allergies, weaker eyesight, exceptionally vivid dreams and so on.

WHAT TO READ AT 3.00 A.M.

'JUST you wait, you'll never have time to read a book again!' So the doom-mongers gleefully declare as soon as one announces one is pregnant. But like a thousand other clichés of motherhood (you'll *never* again have a good night's sleep, you'll *never* again be able to wear a bikini) in some cases it is true, but in some cases it is not. For those lucky mothers whose babies do settle into some kind of standard routine along the lines of feeding for half an hour every three hours, this half hour adds up to more time for reading than at possibly any other time in one's life.

The only trouble is, much of this reading is done at night, which brings with it challenges of its own. If your partner is unable to sleep with the light on, you will need to buy one of those reading lights advertised in the back of the *Sunday Times* magazine. Alternatively, invest in an iPhone or iPad, which are completely brilliant in the dark until the moment your baby gets old enough to be too distracted by them to concentrate on the matter at hand, at which point they become a disaster.

The next question is what to read. It needs to be a text that works well when read in ten-, twenty- or forty-minute doses, depending on how efficient an eater your baby is. Glossy magazines are out of the question for the new mother, since it is indisputable that the more of these one reads, the more inadequate and depressed one feels. So books it is. Not a biography, because one keeps forgetting who all the supporting players are. Ditto nothing with too complicated a plot, so no Charles Dickens or Wilkie Collins or even Penny Vincenzi or Sophie Kinsella: your reading is done in such short chunks that by the time you reach the end of a chapter, you have completely forgotten who left whom what in his will anyway. If you must choose a novel, make sure it is one that is so beautifully written that it doesn't matter if you are unable to remember who any of the characters are; you'll enjoy it sentence by sentence anyway while your baby chomps away. Short stories are OK – for example, Anton Chekhov or Mollie Panter-Downes – but even then you might not make it through to the end without interruption. The perfect solution? Letters (for example, Jane Carlyle or Nancy Mitford) or diaries (for example, Vere Hodgson or Virginia Woolf — though remember, the latter's end badly).

Novels specifically about pregnancy, birth or babies — at least, those not written in the most unbearably sentimental way — are few and far between. Perhaps those in the know are too busy creating great human beings to create great art. There are a few exceptions, though, such as *The Squire* by Enid Bagnold (1938), which is about a forty-four-year-old upper-middle-class woman who is pregnant with her fifth child while her husband is away in India. The climax of the novel is the birth scene, written from the point of view of the participant rather than the onlooker (a near-revolutionary approach in an era when almost the only factual account of birth that was available was the 1933 textbook *Natural Childbirth* by Grantly Dick-Read).

'So it was you!' said the squire to him [her newborn baby], thinking of her nine months' companion, of her hardness towards him, now melted, of his quirks and movements to which she had grown so used, and thinking with wonderment, 'So it was *you*.'

Also fascinating is *The Millstone* by Margaret Drabble (1965), which is about the woes that befall an unmarried academic who gets pregnant in 1960s London. It includes some haunting period details about the workings of the early NHS, including the way that single mothers were routinely referred to as 'Mrs' rather than 'Miss' by midwives and always had to have a sign with the letter 'U' on it hanging from their hospital bed to denote their marital status.

Beware, though. Somebody somewhere will try to make you feel guilty about reading while you feed the baby. This is because there has been the occasional 'expert' over the years who has decreed that if you do not stare into your baby's eyes non-stop for the entire first year of its life, eventually you will be punished for it by ending up with a stupid, miserable child. Clearly, this is complete balls. And anyway, even if it does mean you are a beastly, horrible mother, at least you're not a brain-dead, depressed one with nothing to talk about but the colour of diddums' poo. Still, if you want to hedge your bets, try reading aloud to the baby instead: as long as you do it in a suitably sing-song tone of voice, s/he won't care whether you're reading *Pride and Prejudice* or *Pride and Peekaboo*.

THE SEVEN PRINCIPAL PLAYERS IN THE FIELD OF CHILD DEVELOPMENT

JOHN BOWLBY (1907–90)

Who?	Son of a pathologist. Later director of the World Health Organization.
What?	An attachment theorist. Considers the satisfaction of the human infant's desperation for a secure relationship with adult caregivers imperative, if optimal social and emotional development is to occur.
Why?	Babies are evolved to instinctively hang from and suckle their mothers. Separation signals abandonment and, ultimately, doom. A baby banks on his or her mother and her conscientious responses to sort out and come to know his or her own emotions. Crumbs.
In practice?	Heed the 'maternal instinct', for a mother's response is programmed to buttress infant survival. 'Crying it out' and 'cultivating independence' are

against nature, and the cost is psychological damage.
All round.

The view from here?   Fine, for those who harbour patience levels to rival
Mother Teresa.

JEAN PIAGET (1896–1980)

Who?   A Swiss philosopher-cum-psychologist.

What?   His tedious 'operational stages' harp on about the
laborious accrual of skills of logic and reasoning,
seeking to describe a system of states comprising
child development.

Why?   From birth to the age of two, infants understand the
world through information gleaned from the senses
and movement. This stage is carved up into six
sub-stages, beginning with 'simple reflexes' and
culminating in 'internalization of schemes'. You
were warned.

In practice?   During this stage, children are utterly egocentric
and, for many observers, pretty dull. Just give them
an old Evian bottle and a spoon and let them get on
with it.

The view from here?   Dull, frankly. For those looking for a little more
pizzazz, look no further than . . .

SIGMUND FREUD (1856–1939)

Who?   Austrian neurologist and father of psychoanalysis.

What?   Psychoanalysis works from the premise that psychological nasties in adulthood are rooted in unresolved
conflicts (often involving incestuous fantasies –
squirm) from particular stages of infancy.

Why?   Every stage of a baby's development is directly

related to evolving psychological and bodily needs. The oral stage runs from birth to around eighteen months – hence the intensity of the suckling drive in newborn babies. Freud postulated that an infant's oral focus not only satisfies their nutritional requirements but also provides pleasure.

In practice? Freud believed parents' handling of their offspring during each developmental stage has a profound impact on the blanket development of the child's psyche. Getting stuck at one of these messy phases can lead to awfully embarrassing consequences for the adult self. Concealing overt disgust at baby's emissions should go some way to preventing distasteful fetishes.

The view from here? Rock 'n' roll!

DONALD WINNICOTT (1896–1971)

Who? Worked as a paediatrician and child psychoanalyst for forty years, and famously postulated that a baby exists only as part of a relationship: 'There is no such thing as a baby, only a baby and someone,' he said.

What? He provided meticulous descriptions of what happens between the mutually adapted mother and infant (when breastfeeding, or when a mother cuddles her baby, for instance). Winnicott's theory of the 'good enough' mother (1953) does not refer to the person who succeeds in scraping herself out of bed for the eighteenth feed that night, but to one whose emotional harmony with her baby adapts alongside the differing stages of infancy. The 'good enough mother', believe it or not, does a better job than the 'perfect' one, who risks quashing her child's development as a separate entity. It is official: even attempting to be Wonderwoman is not only harmful but also dangerous.

119

In practice?	Winnicott insisted that no one else can nurture a baby as well as its own mother (cementing any career woman's sense of guilt). By answering the baby's physical and emotional needs, a mother facilitates the seeds of its self-development. During the early stages of his life, little Johnny is at the mercy of innumerable sensations from inside and out, which threaten to besiege him. Winnicott felt that these experiences are potentially terrifying for the newborn baby, unless the baby is 'held' by the primary carer. Not just in a physical sense, but through the parent's containment of those feelings intolerable to the infant. That means not screaming back at the colicky angel.
The view from here?	Have another glass of wine and rope in a pal to do some cuddling. Of the baby. And perhaps you.

MELANIE KLEIN (1882–1960)

Who?	A British psychoanalyst (though born in Austria), and the first practitioner to employ traditional psychoanalysis in work with young children.
What?	According to Klein, a baby feels overwhelmed from birth by untenable 'persecutory' angst, experienced as a consequence of its own physical needs, combined with the many external impediments to those requirements. A rudimentary defence network, consisting of such horrors as 'withdrawal' and 'projection', characterizes the infant's attempts to distinguish itself from the world around it, based on its relationship with the primary beloved and frustrating object, the mother's breast. Well, what else?
In practice?	Regardless of one's beatific smiles and besotted gazes, it seems one's engorged udders are the only part of a

mother a baby has eyes (and feelings) for. Cupboard love (and hate) are what this game is all about, and one may as well resign oneself to it, as all this ardour and rage are crucial to a child's realization that mummy (and all humans) is both lovely and horrid.

The view from here? It's all about the breasts.

ANNA FREUD (1895–1982)

Who? Freud's daughter! She dissociated herself from the somewhat constraining position of her father (without getting too 'psychosexual'), to underscore the conflict endured by the self whilst it attempts to accommodate objectionable, chiefly unconscious, desires alongside the requirements of reality.

What? Anna Freud's research generated the idea of developmental lines, which amalgamated her father's 'primitive drive' model (infants as little mad animals) with an accent on the significance of parents for child development. This concept demonstrated the impact of babies' interior structures, as well as their environment, on how they turn out. Despite allegedly professing happiness that she herself did not have children, Anna Freud drew attention to the value of observation of babies with their parents. Mercifully, however, she suggested that conflicts are inescapable for all children during their self-development, and that not all require professional attention.

In practice? So does your baby need therapy? Freud Jr's position is that if parents avoid downbeat responses to the child's conflicts, probably not. She concluded that families should only really struggle with emotional commotion when, for instance, the mother's emotional focus is directed elsewhere. Fear not, however: it is (almost) certain that shoe-shopping expeditions are not what she had in mind.

The view from here? Well, it does seem a bit early to march them off to therapy. They don't know they're born (ha ha).

WILLIAM RONALD DODDS FAIRBAIRN (1889–1964)

Who? Trained in medicine, Fairbairn was accepted as a member of the British Psychoanalytical Society in 1931. He had the notion that, when a baby's emotional needs are not fulfilled by its parents, a pathological aversion to reality takes root.

What? Fairbairn envisaged the infant as introjecting those insufficient aspects of the parents. For example, when a mother feels anger but works to deny it, her child cannot fully relate to her. The baby instead connects with this repressed characteristic of the parent, and becomes aggressive itself. Fairbairn postulated that our primary connections mould the psychological life of a baby in such a powerful way that they become the blueprint for all adult acquainting. So, when the child starts cavorting with Hell's Angels, or bringing Nick Griffin home for tea . . .

In practice? Whoa. How are we to know whether or not we are meeting the Tiny Emperor's every psychological need? Fairbairn seems to suggest that unstinting responsiveness is what is called for. Do not let the polished, 'dinner party'-style attentiveness that has fooled so many fail one now.

The view from here? More gin, anyone?

SWADDLING

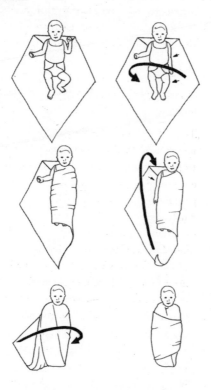

JEAN-JACQUES Rousseau strongly disapproved of swaddling. He believed it was restrictive. But for those who can find the courage to question the highly dubious advice of an eighteenth-century Swiss philosopher who abandoned all five of his illegitimate children to be raised in a foundling hospital, it is to be noted that swaddling is in fact an essential skill to apply to newborns. The more they fight it, the more it means they need it: left to their own devices, they will wake themselves up every half an hour by hitting themselves in the face over and over again like a drunken floozy. Not fun.

'THAT DELUSION CALLED CHICKEN-BROTH'; OR, MRS BEETON'S BREASTFEEDING DIET

The mother, while suckling, as a general rule, should avoid all sedentary occupations, take regular exercise, keep her mind as lively and pleasingly occupied as possible, especially by music and singing. Her diet should be light and nutritious, with a proper sufficiency of animal food, and of that kind which yields the largest amount of nourishment; and, unless the digestion is naturally strong, vegetables and fruit should form a very small proportion of the general dietary, and such preparations as broths, gruels, arrowroot, &c., still less. Tapioca, or ground-rice pudding, made with several eggs, may be taken freely; but all soups and thin potations, such as that delusion called chicken-broth, should be avoided, as yielding a very small amount of nutriment, and a large proportion of flatulence. All purely stimulants should be avoided as much as possible, especially spirits, unless taken for some special object, and that medicinally; but as part of the dietary they should be carefully shunned. Lactation is always an exhausting process, and as the child increases in size and strength, the drain upon the mother becomes great and depressing. Then something more even than an abundant diet is required to keep the mind and body up to a standard sufficiently healthy to admit of a constant and nutritious secretion being performed without detriment to the physical integrity of the mother, or injury to the child who imbibes it; and as stimulants are inadmissible, if not positively injurious, the substitute required is to be found in *malt liquor*. To the lady accustomed to her Madeira and sherry, this may appear a very vulgar potation for a delicate young mother to take instead of the more subtle and condensed elegance of wine; but as we are writing from experience, and with the avowed object of imparting useful facts and beneficial remedies to our readers, we allow no social distinctions to interfere with our legitimate object . . .

As the best tonic, then, and the most efficacious indirect stimulant that a mother can take at such times, there is no potation equal to *porter* and *stout*, or, what is better still, an equal part of porter and stout . . .

Independently of its invigorating influence on the constitution, porter exerts a marked and specific effect on the secretion of milk, more powerful in exciting an abundant supply of that fluid than any other article within the range of the physician's art . . . The quantity to be taken must depend upon the natural strength of the mother, the age and demand made by the infant of the parent, and other causes; but the amount should vary from *one* to *two* pints a day, never taking less than half a pint at a time, which should be repeated three or four times a day . . .

Mrs Beeton's Book of Household Management (1861)

TOP SIX NATURAL REMEDIES FOR A
NEWBORN THAT ACTUALLY WORK

Symptom	Treatment
Nappy rash	If the rash is severe, do not use wipes when changing the nappy. Instead, fill a squirt bottle with lukewarm water mixed with a little bit of baking soda, use it to rinse off the affected area, and then dry with a hairdryer set to cool. Next, apply a cream or oil. Try out a few to see which works for one's own baby, but any zinc oxide cream is to be highly recommended (especially the Burt's Bees one), as is evening primrose oil (just pierce a capsule and apply) or even olive oil straight from the kitchen. The latter will often have worked by the time you next change the nappy. As a preventative measure, a nightly bath in baking soda works wonders, as does an occasional sprinkling of cornstarch.
A cold, cough or croup	Try all of the following: place a humidifier in the room, or alternatively a bowl of water near a radiator; fill the bathroom full of steam and then sit there with the baby for ten minutes; elevate the cot by shoving a couple of books underneath one end of the mattress. Saline drops are also great for unblocking a stuffy little nose.
Cradle cap	Rub olive oil into the scalp and leave it on for as long as you don't mind your baby smelling of a cheap Italian restaurant.
Eczema	Add porridge oats to the baby's bath water (though make sure you wash it off, which can be a hassle). Add lots of flax seed oil to the diet (and/or to the breastfeeding mother's diet), and also try rubbing it directly on the skin.
Constipation	Add flax seed oil to the baby's diet. If lurid green poo is the problem in a breastfed baby, this means the baby is ingesting too high a proportion of fore milk as opposed to hind milk. To solve this, try to make him or her stay longer on each boob before switching.
Ear infection	Rub garlic oil on the ear.

Alternatively, try a centuries-old method: leeches. Custom decreed that these were placed on the baby's head for cradle cap, on the nose for a cold, on the windpipe for croup and on the abdomen and rectum for constipation. Yikes.

BRINGING UP BABY

ALONG with *Birth: The Surprising History of How We Are Born* by Tina Cassidy (2006), Christina Hardyment's brilliant book *Dream Babies: Childcare Advice from John Locke to Gina Ford* (2007) ought to be compulsory reading for mothers-to-be. James Nelson's *Essay on the Government of Children* (1753) was Britain's first comprehensive childcare manual, and this was followed by a veritable onslaught of bossy do's and don'ts. Oh, how quickly fashions in baby rearing change! For instance, as recently as the 1980s it was common for doctors to recommend giving a baby sedatives if s/he did not sleep through the night. Today this would be severely frowned upon, not least because any fool knows that it is surely far more sensible to give the sedatives to the mother. Anyway, below are a few more gems from the history of childcare advice.

ON HOW TO CHOOSE A WET NURSE

> Chuse one of middle age, nor old nor young,
> Nor plump nor slim her make, but firm and strong,
> Upon her cheek let health refulgent glow

In vivid colours, that good humour show;
Long be her arms, and broad her amply chest;
Her neck be finely tuned and full her breast:
Let the twin hills be white as mountain snow,
Their swelling veins with circling juices flow;
Each in a well-projecting nipple end,
And milk in copious streams from these descend:
This the delighted babe will instant chose,
And he knows best what quantity to use.

Scévole de Sainte Marthe, *Paedotrophia* (1585)

ON THE IMPORTANCE OF COLD BATHS

A great deal in providing for the health and strength of children
depends on their being duly and daily washed, when well, in cold
water from head to foot. Their cries testify to what degree they
dislike this. They squall and twist and kick about at a fine rate, and
many mothers, too many, neglect this, partly from reluctance to
encounter the squalling, and partly, much too often, from what I
will not call idleness, but to which I cannot apply a milder term
than neglect. Well and duly performed it is an hour's good tight
work; for besides the bodily labour, which is not very slight when
the child gets to be five or six months old, there is the singing to
overpower the voice of the child.

William Cobbett, *Advice to Young Men and Incidentally*
Young Women on How to be a Father

ON CRYING

A babe can only express his wants and his necessities by a cry; he can only tell his aches and his pains by a cry; it is the only language of babyhood; it is the most ancient of all languages; it is the language known by our earliest progenitors; it is, if listened to aright, a very expressive language, although it is only but the language of a cry —

'Soft infancy, that nothing canst but cry.' — *Shakespeare*

There is, then, a language in the cry of an infant, which to a mother is the most interesting of all languages . . . The cry of passion, for instance, is a furious cry; the cry of sleepiness is a drowsy cry; the cry of grief is a sobbing cry; the cry of an infant when roused from sleep is a shrill cry; the cry of hunger is very characteristic, — it is unaccompanied with tears, and is a wailing cry; the cry of teething is a fretful cry; the cry of pain tells to the practised ear the part of pain . . . a cry, at night, for light — a frequent cause of a baby crying — is a restless cry:-

'An infant crying in the night;

An infant crying for the light:

And with no language by a cry.' — *Tennyson*.

Pye Henry Chavasse, *Advice to a Wife* (1868)

ON THE BABY BLUES

She is more perplexed than pleased, more frightened than delighted, by the young person who develops such extraordinary powers of harassment that one wonders not only how one lived through the tremendous anxieties of birth; but how one is to live under the weight of alarm and responsibility which is suddenly placed on our shoulder . . . The dreams that a young mother is supposed to dream over the cradle of her new-born baby are about as real as her supposedly passionate desire for children. She dreams principally about herself, she longs to be out of bondage. A little indignant at the manner in which the child engrosses everyone's time and attention, the while she is abjectly terrified of it, and as abjectly afraid that everyone who touches it will do it a mischief . . . Those thoughts may not be noble, but they are universal, and therefore the girl who feels them agitating her breast need not write herself down a monster — the phase will soon pass.

Mrs Panton, *The Way They Should Go* (1896)

ON THE IMPORTANCE OF FRESH AIR

The importance of fresh air cannot be overrated. Children who always have enough of it *never catch colds*. It is the coddled children, the children accustomed to hot rooms and to too many garments, who are always being kept indoors with 'streaming colds'.

But fresh air does not mean draughts, and does not involve the constant changes of temperature to which so many unfortunate children are subjected.

In winter children should never be in a heated room — should never see a fire — until they come in for good at tea-time . . .

Infants (as soon as they are acclimatized to this world) and older children should be out all day *in all weathers* except fog, or in some special cases a severe east wind, though the average healthy child is generally unaffected by the latter. But '*in and out all day*' *means danger*. The greater the contrast between the warmth inside and the cold outside, the greater the danger.

Infants should hardly be indoors at all between 8 in the morning and 5 at night in the winter, and from 7am to 10pm in the summer. The breast-fed baby must come indoors for meals, but the bottle or spoon-fed baby should be indoors *only* for dressing and undressing . . .

The amount of time spent by the average child out-of-doors in the winter is from three to four hours. *It should be seven.* There is no reason why a baby who still sleeps before tea should not sleep out in the dark. If possible (and a very little management should make it possible) every child should have a brisk run before breakfast. This expands the lungs, stimulates the appetite, and tones up the whole system . . .

Meals should be eaten out-of-doors whenever possible. A bottle-fed baby should have all feeds outside . . . *Remember that the colder the day the more risky will it be to let the baby have his dinner in a warm room.*

. . . Strong cages are now made that can be attached outside windows, making available even for the flat-dweller every minute of the precious sunshine. They must be fastened in by a builder . . .

Mrs Frankenburg, *Common Sense in the Nursery* (1922)

ON ROUTINE

Truby King babies are fed four-hourly from birth, with few exceptions, and they do not have any nightfeeds. A Truby King baby has as much fresh air and sunshine as possible, and the right amount of sleep . . . He sleeps and kicks out of doors as much as the weather allows, and sleeps at night in the airiest bedroom, or on an open veranda or porch, being carefully protected by a screen to keep him from draughts. After he has gone through his regular morning performance of bathing and being 'held out', and has had breakfast, he sleeps all morning. If he wakes a little before his 2pm meal, all that one knows about it is a suddenly glimpsed chubby little leg or foot waved energetically from his cot for inspection, or a vigorous jerking of the pram.

Mary Truby King, *Mothercraft* (1934)

The above-mentioned *Mothercraft* was the manual most used by our grandmother's generation, just as *Baby and Child Care* by Benjamin Spock (1946), which propounds an altogether more *laissez-faire* approach ('Trust yourself. You know more than you think you do'), was by far the most popular one among our mothers' generation.

The reason you read childcare manuals is that you hope one of them will reveal the secret to programming your baby like a DVR. The trouble, however, with reading too many of them is that they have a horrible way of overriding your instincts with doubt, constant doubt. So instead it is far better to turn to the science of how a baby's brain develops. Try *What's Going On In There?* by Lise Eliot (1999), *Why Love Matters* by Sue Gerhardt (2004) or *Bright from the Start* by Jill Stamm (2007) (all terrible titles, all very good books). Here is what most of them boil down to: the key to helping your baby grow up to be a happy as well as clever individual is to talk to them. A lot. Whilst looking them in the eye. Oh, and hug them as much as possible too. There. Cheque please.

Alternatively, just ask yourself, 'What would Madonna do?' It works when choosing an outfit, so why on earth would it not work for taking care of a baby?

BLOWING ON A BABY'S FACE . . .

. . . is funny. Go on: try it. In addition, as a desperate, last resort it almost always stops a baby crying: it won't last for long, but you will have at least three magical seconds of silence while the baby tries to work out what is going on and where that draft came from.

TO REUSE OR NOT TO REUSE? THAT IS THE (VERY TRICKY) QUESTION

WHAT sort of nappies to use is a tricky issue indeed for any well-intentioned new mother. In an attempt to settle the matter once and for all, in 2008 the British government's Environment Agency published a report into the environmental impact of disposable nappies in comparison to reusable cloth nappies (revised from the original 2006 version, which was found to have various flaws). Here are its (rather inconclusive) conclusions :

The study has estimated, using a 2006 reference point, the environmental impacts of a child using disposable nappies for the first two and a half years of its life and a child using shaped cloth nappies for the same period.

The study demonstrates the environmental effects of:

— Disposable nappy design and manufacturing.
— Disposable nappy disposal choices.
— Laundry choices for shaped cloth nappy use.

The average 2006 disposable nappy would result in a global warming impact of approximately 550kg of carbon dioxide equivalents used over the two and a half years a child is typically in nappies. The global warming impact from disposable nappies use has decreased since the previous study due to manufacturing changes and a 13.5 per cent reduction in the weight of nappies.

The report highlights that the manufacture of disposable nappies has greater environmental impact in the UK than their waste management by landfill.

For reusable nappies, the baseline scenario based on average washer and drier use produced a global warming impact of approximately 570kg of carbon dioxide equivalents. However, the study showed that the impacts for reusable nappies are highly dependent on the way they are laundered.

Washing the nappies in fuller loads or line drying them outdoors all the time (ignoring UK climatic conditions for the purposes of illustration) was found to reduce this figure by 16 per cent. Combining three of the beneficial scenarios (washing nappies in a fuller load, outdoor line drying all of the time, and reusing nappies on a second child) would lower the global warming impact by 40 per cent from the baseline scenario, or some 200kg of carbon dioxide equivalents over the two and a half years, equal to driving a car approximately 1,000 km.

In contrast, the study indicated that if a consumer tumble-dried all their reusable nappies, it would produce a global warming impact 43 per cent higher than the baseline scenario. Similarly, washing nappies at 90°C instead of at 60°C would increase global warming impact by 31 per cent over the baseline. Combining these two energy intensive scenarios would increase the global warming impact by 75 per cent over the baseline scenario, or some 420kg of carbon dioxide equivalent over the two and a half years.

*The environmental impacts of using shaped reusable nappies can be higher or lower than using disposables, depending on how they are laundered. The report shows that, in contrast to the use of disposable nappies, it is consumers' behaviour after purchase that determines most of the impacts from reusable nappies.**

---

* Author's italics.

Cloth nappy users can reduce their environmental impacts by:
— Line drying outside whenever possible.
— Tumble drying as little as possible.
— When replacing appliances, choosing more energy efficient appliances (A+ rated machines are preferred).
— Not washing above 60°C.
— Washing fuller loads.
— Reusing nappies on other children.

Source: *An Updated Lifecycle Assessment Study for Disposable and Reusable nappies*
(Environment Agency, October 2008)

ALL ABOUT MARY CASSATT

MARY Cassatt (1844–1926) was born in Pennsylvania, the daughter of a stockbroker. In 1874, at the age of thirty, she moved to Paris and lived there for the rest of her life; 'After all give me France — women do not have to fight for recognition here, if they do serious work,' she wrote to a friend. Before long the painter Edgar Degas had become something of a mentor to her, and he drew her into the circle of Impressionist painters who were just beginning to make their mark on the world's art scene. While Cassatt chose not to have children herself (or even get married), she loved to paint them, and from about 1890 they became almost the sole subject of her art. Consider, therefore, buying a poster or postcard of one of her (moving, beautiful, unusual) paintings of babies to vivify your own baby's room. Those that date from the period after 1900 show Cassatt truly at the peak of her talents, and here is a list of most of them.

Title	Medium	Date	Current location
Jules Dried by His Mother	Oil on canvas	1901	Anonymous collection, Middlebury, Connecticut
Woman in Red Bodice and her Child	Oil on canvas	1901	Brooklyn Museum, Brooklyn, New York
Children Playing with Their Mother	Pastel on paper	1901	Anonymous collection
Sara Handing a Toy to the Baby	Oil on canvas	c.1901	Hill-Stead Museum, Farmington, Connecticut
Mother, Sara, and the Baby	Pastel	c.1901	Hal Wallis, California
Sara and Her Mother with the Baby (No. 1)	Pastel	c.1901	Mrs Burton Carter, Fort Worth, Texas
Sara and Her Mother with the Baby (No. 2)	Oil on canvas	c.1901	Anonymous collection, Paris, France
Sara and Her Mother Admiring the Baby	Pastel on paper	c.1901	Anonymous collection, Buffalo, New York
Woman with Baby	Pastel on paper	1902	Sterling and Francine Clark Art Institute, Williamstown, Massachusetts
Woman in an Orange Wrapper Holding Her Nude Baby	Pastel on grey paper	1902	Anonymous collection, New York, New York
Sketch of Reine with a Nude Baby Leaning Against Her	Pastel on grey paper	c.1902	Mrs David Marman, Kansas City, Missouri
Reine Lefebvre with Blond Baby and Sara Holding a Cat	Pastel on paper	c.1902	Mr and Mrs Sidney Rabb, Boston, Massachusetts
Study of Reine Lefebvre Holding a Nude Baby	Oil on canvas	c.1902	Anonymous collection, Paris, France
Nude Baby Beside Her Mother	Pastel on paper	c.1902	Unlocated
Study of the Baby for The Caress	Pastel on paper	c.1902	Mr and Mrs Danny Kaye, Beverly Hills, California

Title	Medium	Date	Current location
Reine Lefebvre Holding a Nude Baby	Oil on canvas	1902–3	Worcester Art Museum, Worcester, Massachusetts
Tondo Mural for Harrisburg Statehouse	Oil on canvas	1905	Mrs Percy C. Madeira, Berwyn, Pennsylvania
Mother Kissing Her Baby on the Forehead While He Holds His Foot	Oil on canvas	c.1906	Unlocated
Mother and Child in a Landscape with a Friend Admiring the Baby	Watercolour on paper	c.1906	Sotheby Parke Bernet, New York, New York
Stout Mother Trying to Awake Her Baby	Pastel on paper	c.1907	Galerie Jean Tiroche, Palm Beach, Florida
Young Mother and Two Children	Oil on canvas	1908	White House, Washington, DC
Tendresse Maternelle (Mother Jean Embracing her Baby)	Pastel	1908	Seattle Art Museum, Seattle, Washington
Sketch of Mother Jeanne Nursing Her Baby	Oil on canvas	c.1908	Unlocated
Sketch of Mother Jeanne Looking Down at Her Baby	Pastel and crayon on tan board	c.1908	Unlocated
Sketch of Mother and Daughter Looking at the Baby	Pastel on grey paper	c.1908	Maier Museum of Art, Lynchburg, Virginia
Baby Smiling at Two Young Women	Oil on linen	c.1908	Unlocated
Baby Asleep on Mother's Shoulder	Watercolour on white paper	c.1908	Durand-Ruel, Paris, France
Sketch of Dark-haired Mother with Her Baby at Left	Watercolour on paper	c.1908	Mr and Mrs Maurice Fulton, Glencoe, Illinois

Title	Medium	Date	Current location
Sketch of Mother Jeanne Looking down, with Her Baby (No. 1)	Watercolour on paper	c.1908	Mrs Alvin J. Walker, Montreal, Canada
Sketch of Mother Jeanne Looking down, with Her Baby (No. 3)	Watercolour on paper	c.1908	Mr and Mrs Gerald Bronfman, Montreal, Canada
New Brother	Pastel	c.1908	Mr and Mrs John Nichols, Newport Beach, California
Femme et Enfant	Watercolour on paper	c.1908	Dr and Mrs A.G. Ramos, Kansas City, Missouri
Mother Holding a Nude Baby Playing with a Toy Duck	Oil on canvas	1909	Chauncy Stillman, Amenia, New York
Mother in Profile with Baby Cheek to Cheek (No. 2)	Oil on canvas	c.1909	John L. Roper II, Norfolk, Virginia
Mother Wearing a Pink Dress Holding Her Nude Baby Outdoors	Oil on canvas	c.1909	M. Poirier, Paris, France
Mother in a Large Hat Holding Her Nude Baby Seen in Back View	Oil on canvas	c.1909	Joseph King, New York, New York
Mother in Profile with Baby Cheek to Cheek (No. 1)	Pastel on paper	c.1909	Anonymous collection, Great Neck, New York
Baby John Nursing	Pastel	1910	Parke-Bernet Galleries, New York, New York
Baby John with Forefinger in His Mouth	Pastel on grey paper	1910	Yale University Art Gallery, New Haven, Connecticut
Baby John with His Mother	Pastel	c.1910	Metropolitan Museum of Art
Sleepy Baby	Pastel on paper	c.1910	Dallas Museum of Art, Dallas, Texas

Title	Medium	Date	Current location
Baby John Asleep Sucking His Thumb	Pastel	c.1910	Mr and Mrs Richard Pfeil, Indianapolis, Indiana
Baby John and His Mother: Two Heads	Watercolour on paper	c.1910	Unlocated
Sketch of Baby and His Mother	Watercolour on paper	c.1910	Durand-Ruel, Paris, France
Baby John on His Mother's Lap	Pastel on paper	c.1910	Fisher Governor Foundation, Marshalltown, Iowa
Bébé Souriant à Sa Mère	Pastel on paper	1913	Westmoreland Museum of Art, Greensburg, Pennsylvania
Nude Baby on Mother's Lap Resting Her Right Arm on the Back of a Chair	Pastel on paper	1913	Harris J. Klein, New York, New York
Mother in Striped Head Scarf Embraced by Her Baby	Pastel on paper mounted on canvas	1914	Metropolitan Museum of Art, New York, New York
Mother about to Kiss her Baby	Pastel on paper	c.1914	Stephen Hahn Gallery, New York, New York
Baby Lying on His Mother's Lap Reaching to Hold a Scarf	Pastel on brown paper	c.1914	Mr and Mrs Philip D. Sang
Baby Sucking His Finger While Held by His Mother	Pastel on paper	c.1914	Unlocated
Mother Holding Her Nude Baby Whose Left Hand Rests on the Mother's Chest	Pastel on paper	c.1914	Sotheby Parke Bernet, New York, New York
Slight Sketch of Back View of Mother and Baby	Pastel on paper	c.1914	Mme de la Chapelle, Paris, France
Mother Seated with a Baby Standing Next to Her in a Landscape	Oil on canvas	c.1914	Unlocated

Source: Smithsonian Institution

HOW TO TAKE A BABY'S TEMPERATURE

FIRST of all, if your baby feels hot to the touch, do not panic. A temperature is the body's way of trying to fight off a virus, so in a way it is a positive sign and only a problem if it turns out to be a symptom of something else or if it is making the baby excessively uncomfortable.

Still, it is always best to check. Hopefully you already own a (digital, not mercury) thermometer, so that you will not have to race around town searching for a twenty-four-hour chemist at which to buy one: it is almost always the middle of the night when one suddenly needs one, which is not a coincidence, since a baby's temperature does indeed rise at night.

Be mindful of the fact that the baby needs to be relatively calm when you take her (or his) temperature, since crying will artificially inflate the reading. There are three methods that can be used on babies: in the ear, under the arm or up the bottom. In the ear is the least reliable of all, giving inflated readings as though designed to panic you. Up the bottom — rectally, as it is technically known— is the most accurate, but is difficult to obtain, painful and risky on a wriggly baby; hence it is really only an option for the very trained or the very brave. So under the arm it is.

Remove the baby's clothes. Place the thermometer under the baby's armpit and then hold her arm firmly down over it to keep it in place. Frantically distract your baby as best you can (or ideally get someone else to while you concentrate on keeping the thermometer in place). Most thermometers beep when ready to read, which is normally within about sixty seconds: this feels like for ever when you are trying to keep a baby still, but is actually relatively quick compared to the time taken by older models.

Here's how to interpret the thermometer's reading when taken under the arm:

36–37°C:	Normal.
38°C or higher:	A bit of a temperature. If your baby is younger than three months, call the doctor; if your baby of any age also has cold hands or feet along with a temperature, call 999.
39°C or higher:	A proper temperature. If your baby is younger than six months, call the doctor.
40°C or higher:	A high temperature. Call the doctor.

However, it is not so much about the number as about other out-of-the-ordinary symptoms: not eating, sleeping more than usual, vomiting, breathing difficulties, a temperature that persists for several days. If, aside from the temperature, your baby does not seem out of sorts, there is rarely reason to worry. If in any doubt at all, though, be sure to ring NHS Direct or your GP, or go to A&E.

Then get the baby back to sleep, get into bed and lie awake and worry until morning.

BREASTFEEDING À LA MODE

ACCORDING to the Department of Health, by the time a baby is six weeks old only 48 per cent of mothers are still indulging in a little of *l'allaitement maternel* — or, as it is also more prosaically known, breastfeeding. By the time six months have passed, this figure has dropped to 25 per cent, while the number of little ones for whom this is the sole sort of nutrition on the menu constitutes less than I per cent. There is a major reason for this that has thus far gone all but undocumented: that is, the dizzying number of fashion conundrums that breastfeeding presents.

It is to be noted that even some of the greatest minds of our time have thus far failed to solve the problem of the breast-feeding bra. The result is that all those on offer are appallingly, shockingly, criminally frumpy. The least bad option looks-wise is the Elle Macpherson range, but just because they have a label with a supermodel's name stitched in them, do not be fooled into thinking that they will make you look like her. They will not. They also have another disadvantage: they are worth considering only on the understanding that the way they are constructed seems to encourage one's breasts to sag so far that one trips over them at every pirouette. So those who, for some strange reason, object to this would do well to consider instead the Bravado Body Silk Nursing Bra, which is one of the few with enough built-in padding to conceal one's breastpads. For surely breast-pads (note even the plodding cadence of the word itself) are the least glamorous entity known to mankind, the veritable Ken Barlow of underwear products. Alternatively, it is actually perfectly possible to whip one's breasts out when wearing a standard Agent Provocateur bra. The regular squidging out of shape of the bra that this entails does cause it some long-term damage, but consider it worth it.

Night-time presents sartorial problems of its own. Most notable of these is that it is necessary to develop a penchant for pyjamas, which not only offer the baby easy access but are also essential for keeping warm when up in the middle of the night. The purchase of a pair will entirely transform the experience of night feeds. To this end, run – don't waddle – to a Cath Kidston shop. John Lewis also carries surprisingly chic options.

There is no doubt that the act of breastfeeding complicates a number of life's great pleasures. Take swimming in the sea. Built-in padding is again a necessity when considering a swimsuit, so that one's breastpads are not too obvious. Just do not forget to remove them every time the opportunity for a dip in the ocean arises. Unless one is Heidi Klum, a one-piece is probably a given for the new mum; be sure, however, to shun a tankini at all costs. One might just as well wear a sign round one's neck saying 'I Give Up'.

But possibly the most challenging of all outings for the breastfeeding mother is the black-tie do. Options to consider include a dress with ruffles a-plenty (they disguise leaks splendidly), a shirt dress (easy access) or even some sort of shorts suit (ditto, with exceptional flair and fabulousness). If bringing the baby along in a sling, bear in mind that high heels cause one to lose one's balance rather more easily than usual. The Nobel Peace Prize ceremony is mostly sitting down, though, so one is probably fine in even the most uncomfortable shoes. For an all-day event like the Oscars, a breast pump is an indispensable accessory. Thankfully, they tend to come in black to match one's Louboutins. Just hope that no one asks the name of the designer: 'Medela' or 'Avent' will elicit no small number of looks of confusion from the assembled paparazzi.

GROW, KID, GROW

Weight-for-age GIRLS
Birth to 6 months (percentiles)

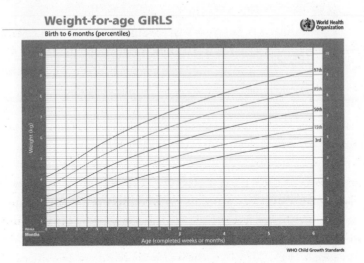

Length-for-age GIRLS
Birth to 6 months (percentiles)

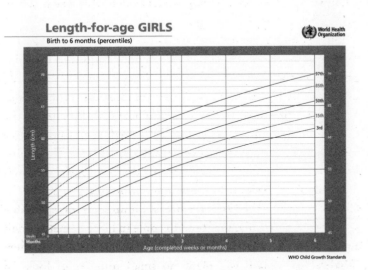

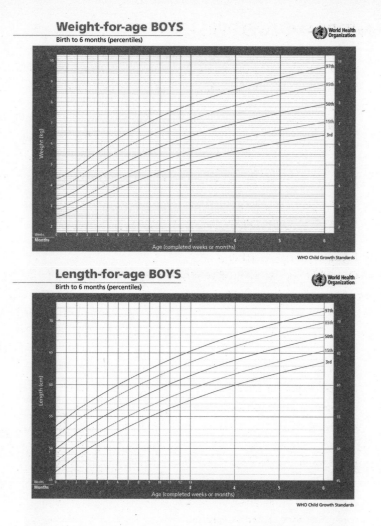

Source: World Health Organization

NB: Since 2006, the World Health Organization has based its calculations of what is 'normal' in terms of a baby's weight and height on breastfed babies. Formula-fed babies will be bigger.

THE PRAM: TWO PERSPECTIVES

Sir.-

I beg leave to draw the attention of the public (I was about to say police) to one of the now existing nuisances. It is that of perambulators. You cannot walk along without meeting several of those novel vehicles; and, as their name implies, they 'walk through' the foot-passenger; for you must either go fairly off the pavement or suffer the more pleasant sensation of having your corns (if you are accompanied by those agreeables) run over.

If it were a truck of apples, instead of children, the police would interfere. Why not in this? Apologizing,

I remain yours respectfully,

One of the inconvenienced public.

The Times, 20 October 1855

You know, I still feel in my wrists certain echoes of the pram-pusher's knack, such as, for example, the glib downward pressure one applied to the handle in order to have the carriage tip up and climb the curb. First came an elaborate mouse-gray vehicle of Belgian make, with fat autoid tires and luxurious springs, so large that it could not enter our puny elevator. It rolled on sidewalks in a slow stately mystery, with the trapped baby inside lying supine, well covered with down, silk and fur; only his eyes moved, warily, and sometimes they turned upward with one swift sweep of their showy lashes to follow the receding of branch-patterned blueness that flowed away from the edge of the half-cocked hood of the carriage, and presently he would dart a suspicious glance at my face to see if the teasing trees and sky did not belong, perhaps, to the same order of things as did rattles and parental humor. There followed a lighter carriage, and in this, as he spun along, he would tend to rise, straining at his straps; clutching at the edges; standing there less like the groggy passenger of a pleasure boat than like an entranced scientist in a spaceship; surveying the speckled skeins of a live, warm world; eyeing with philosophic interest the pillow he had managed to throw overboard; falling out himself when a strap burst one day. Still later he rode in one of those small contraptions called strollers; from initial springy and secure heights the child came lower and lower, until, when he was about one and a half, he touched ground in front of the moving stroller by slipping forward out of his seat and beating the sidewalk with his heels in anticipation of being set loose in some public garden. A new wave of evolution started to swell, gradually lifting him again from the ground, when, for his second birthday, he received a four-foot-long, silver-painted Mercedes racing car operated by inside pedals, like an organ, and in this he used to drive with a pumping, clanking noise up and down the sidewalk of the Kurfurstendamm while from open windows came the multiplied roar of a dictator still pounding his chest in the Neander valley we had left far behind.

Vladimir Nabokov, *Speak, Memory* (1951)

AMIES SANS ENFANTS

MAINTAINING your relationships with your friends who do not have babies can be a minefield. In your world it has become horrifyingly normal to debate the likes of why poo sometimes goes green and how best to ease the pain of haemorrhoids in so loud a tone that every barista within earshot feels all but obliged to join in. In your friend's world, however, it is just more evidence that you have once and for all gone over to the dark side: Motherhood. Here, then, are some tips on how to avoid losing your dear *amie sans enfants* (ASE) for ever.

THE TEN RULES OF ENGAGEMENT

I. *Do not . . .* appear too flippin' furious when ASE turns up forty-five minutes late, leaving you with a mere ten minutes to exchange news before your baby wakes up from his or her extremely carefully timed nap and demands undivided attention. ASE does not intend to be annoying; she (or he) just does not understand. You probably were not Miss Punctuality either in your pre-baby life. Similarly, try not to lose your temper when ASE rings up to cancel with only a moment's notice, even if you have re-jigged your baby's entire sleeping/eating/cooing routine to accommodate the plan. ASE will then try to make up for her flakiness by asking whether she can instead pop round after work at 6 o'clock-ish, which everyone with a baby knows is the absolute worst time of day possible to try to hold a sensible conversation. Again, stay calm, and suggest that on the way over she dilly-dally in Top Shop for an hour or so in the hope that, by the time she does turn up, your baby will finally have conked out for the night and you will be ready to inject yourself with the gin that, if she is any kind of friend at all, she will bring with her for a giggle-filled (but hopefully gurgle-free) evening on the sofa.

2. *Do not* . . . choose any issue related to your baby's bowel movements to be your opening conversational salvo. The colour, the frequency, how strange that the poo smells quite sweet or that you mind much less than you thought you would when you find you have some smeared on your face: all this is the sort of talk that gives mothers everywhere a bad name. If you are really unable to help yourself, at least make the discussion interesting: for example, regale the listener with tales of how Neanderthals used to rub faeces all over their arrows when going into battle, in a deliberate attempt to spread disease.

3. *Do not* . . . expect ASE to coo endlessly over your baby. Unless she really is 'a baby person', it can be jolly hard to know what to say: most babies are not only quite boring but also rather ugly, at least in the eyes of anyone other than very close relations. 'I think very young babies rather disgusting,' wrote Queen Victoria to her daughter in 1872. To avoid awkwardness, arrange to meet somewhere where the ASE is not obliged to have too much interaction with the baby: a busy café or a packed boardroom, perhaps, rather than your own sitting room.

4. *Do not* . . . coo endlessly over your baby yourself. A rule of thumb is to pay the little darling as little attention as you think you can get away with without ASE calling social services. Only change a nappy if you absolutely must. Only feed if it is the

best way to get some peace. Keep cooing, canoodling and kissing to a minimum; this is not the time or the place. You at least want to *trick* ASE into thinking you have not changed too much, don't you?

5. *Do not* . . . make value judgements that appear to belittle those who have made different life choices to you. This may seem an obvious no-no, but in the self-obsessed fog that is new motherhood, it is often forgotten. So, for instance, do not moan about how having a baby is so much harder work than having a job; on the flip side, do not pontificate about how no amount of fancy hotels and expensive shoes and holidays can match the joy of the first time your baby smiles. Such utterances will gain you *nada*.

6. *Do not* . . . rant about how these days the only clothes shopping you do is of the 'smash and grab' variety — that is, where you are in such a hurry that you do not bother to try anything on. There is no point making excuses about what you are wearing; most people do not notice anyway until you draw attention to the fact, since they are too busy worrying about their own appearance. Rather, take the dignified approach and let everyone assume that what you are wearing is your perfect outfit: mucky jeans, sweaty T-shirt, the coat you wore when you were pregnant — darling, the Paris catwalks would be proud. If you do feel obliged to jazz up your look a little, a posh haircut works wonders when it comes to impressing the fashion set.

7. *Do not* . . . allow the phrase 'the miracle of life' to pass your lips. Ever. Sure, having a baby emphasizes 'the miracle of life' to you as nothing else does — it is like having your very own science project right there in your front room — but nobody

other than your partner or *at a pinch* your mum wants to be subjected to such clichés, true or not.

8. *Do not* . . . heap criticism upon mutual friends who also recently became mothers. Admittedly, though, this is often difficult to resist: there is nobody on earth more judgemental of a mother than another mother.

9. *Do not* . . . let your boss hear you talking to ASE or in fact to anyone about your baby. If your boss does ask you directly, 'How's the baby?', 99 per cent of the time the correct answer is a simple 'Very well indeed, thank you for asking', accompanied by a smile fond enough to avoid starting office gossip that you lack maternal instinct, but final enough to preclude further polite enquiries. And that's it. Not a word more. As a legendary female publisher once told one of her authors, when informed that said author was going to be unable to make a five o'clock meeting because that was when her children had their supper: 'Don't talk to me about your fucking children.' It is an exhortation worth remembering.

10. *Do not* . . ., when meeting up after 7.00 p.m., complain about the trials and tribulations you had trying to find a babysitter. First of all, what you mean is trying to find a babysitter you can trust to take care of your precious diddums, since there's always someone available, even if it is the crack-head granny who lives next door. Second of all: to repeat, nobody cares.

In summary, you may not feel normal, but for the love of God at least try to *act* normal. Whatever that means.

THE MOON

Rumour has it that some babies wake up in the night. If yours is not one of them, keep quiet and thank your lucky stars and moons. If s/he is, however, you are destined to spend many a midnight hour staring out the window, frantically trying to rock your darling one to sleep with only the bright shining *luna* for company. So here are a few facts about said *luna* to ponder.

Age of the Moon: 4.6 billion years old.

Origins of the Moon: There are various theories, but most scientists agree that the Moon was formed when the Earth crashed into some other entity the size of a planet. The impact resulted in a huge dust cloud of vaporized rock, which then cooled down and condensed into a ring of solid bodies, which in turn eventually gathered together to create the Moon.

Average radius of the Moon (that is, the distance from its centre to its surface): 1,079.6 miles, which is about a third of the average radius of the Earth.

Mass of the Moon: 8.10 x 1,019 tons.

Density of the Moon: 3.34 grams per cubic centimetre.

Average thickness of the Moon's crust: about 43 miles, which is 37 miles more than the average thickness of the Earth's crust.

Average distance from the centre of the Moon to the centre of the Earth: 238,897 miles, which is about 30 times the diameter of the Earth.

Speed at which the Moon is moving away from the Earth: 1.5 inches each year.

Temperature range at the lunar equator: −173°C (−280°F) at night to 127°C (260°F) in the daytime.

Largest crater on the Moon: the South Pole-Aitken Basin, which is 1,550 miles in diameter.

Name of the light areas visible on the Moon from the Earth: terrae (with the emphasis on the first syllable), which is Latin for 'lands'.

Name of the dark areas visible on the Moon from the Earth: maria (with the emphasis on the first syllable), which is Latin for 'seas'.

Date of the first Moon landing: 20 July 1969.

Composition of the Moon: the core is made of iron, the surface of silicate.

Number of phases of the Moon: four (new moon, first quarter, full moon and last quarter).

Frequency with which a full moon occurs: About every 29 days, which is the duration of one complete lunar cycle. A full moon occurs when the Moon is on the opposite side of the Earth from the Sun, and all three are completely aligned in a straight line. This means that, viewed from the Earth, the near side of the Moon appears fully illuminated.

Amount one would weigh on the Moon, if one weighed 150 pounds on the Earth: 25 pounds, due to gravity being only a sixth of what it is on the Earth.

The year Galileo wrote the first scientific description of the Moon: 1609.

Most recent expedition to the Moon: the *Apollo 17* space mission in 1972.

Likelihood of your baby becoming Prime Minister if given the first name Moon: low.

Likelihood of your baby being able to live on the Moon in fifty years: low to medium.

The folklore: Some claim that the gravitational pull of the Moon affects a pregnant woman's amniotic fluid in just the same way that it affects the water in the Earth's seas and rivers to create tides. This, apparently, is why more babies are born during a full moon than at any other time.

Source: NASA

MONDAY'S CHILD

Monday's child is fair of face,
Tuesday's child is full of grace,
Wednesday's child is full of woe,
Thursday's child has far to go,
Friday's child is loving and giving,
Saturday's child works hard for a living,
But the child who is born on the Sabbath Day
Is bonny and blithe and good and gay.

THE ETIQUETTE OF THE PLAYGROUP

YOU will be exhausted in the weeks following the birth of your baby. Emotional, physical and psychological reserves are at their lowest ebb, and, once your own mother has buzzed off back home and your partner has returned to work, it is easy to feel isolated and blue. But fear not! For there is an underground culture out there of which your pre-pregnant self could scarcely have dreamt. It is a world of languorous lattes and cake-fuelled camaraderie, justified many times over by the heady delights of baby music ('n' 'movement', often), baby massage, baby yoga, baby gym, baby sign language, baby storytime and baby 'bouncing'. Any spurious excuse, frankly, to squeeze cash from desperate new mums who have not yet factored in the opportunity for a shower but know that they must (for both their own sanity and the long-term psychological wellbeing of their offspring) socialize (and to hell with the smell). Some such gatherings are even free of charge, as more and more local government initiatives spring up with the aim of alleviating the post-natal suffering of women, devising schemes to persuade despairing mums of a valid reason to abandon the deceptive comforts of home.

Once coaxed from the single room in which you have been squatting (now turned squalid camp of day-old nappies and sodden breastpads), do ensure that several changes of baby clothes accompany the expeditionary troops, as well as at least one grown-up version. Babies are capable of pooing through three outfits in as many minutes, and it is thoroughly disheartening to make it out into the world, only to have to return home, mission aborted and murderous thoughts in mind, because both of you are now besplattered in dandelion-yellow emissions.

Alternatively, for those seeking to splash the cash, Orla Kiely does a range of clothes (handbags, too) in colours that hide the poo splendidly (this is meant as a compliment, by the way).

Should you miraculously succeed in reaching the intended destination poo-free, take a few deep breaths prior to entering. If possible, check in a mirror (probably no handbag these days; perhaps pop a compact into the bottom of the buggy, if there's still room?) Again, it is dreadful to have come this far and launch oneself at a new, glittering mum-galaxy, only to discover that your hair was laced with sick throughout the entire proceedings.

And now, how best to present yourself and your progeny? With luck, these women could be your comrades for keeps.

THINGS YOU SHOULD DEFINITELY SAY

— 'What a beautiful baby!'
— 'My baby never sleeps, constantly screams, and I'm going mad.'
— 'Does anyone know what to do about weaning/sleeping/ husbands who refuse to change nappies?'
— 'Gosh, you're thin!'
— 'Were you an elder child — you're such a natural with him/her?'
— 'I love your buggy — I wish I'd bought one of those' (especially if it looks particularly expensive).
— 'Of course you don't smell of sick/poo/sweat.'
— 'But are you old enough to have a baby, even?'
— 'Everyone back to mine for lots of cake and gallons of tea!'

- 'But is it a boy or a girl?'
- 'Oh my gosh, did my breast milk just shoot out and hit you in the eye?'
- 'My baby sleeps through the night, and has done since she was born.'
- 'Is that a rash?'
- 'Everything you're doing with your baby is wrong; everything I am doing is correct and the way we all should be doing it.'
- 'Are you doing Weight Watchers? Because it didn't work for me either.'
- 'Well, mine's a Gina [Ford] baby all the way!'
- 'Oh, I don't invite babies back to mine — the mess is unbearable.'

If you do succeed in skirting such pitfalls, chances are the invitations to 'playdates' will come flooding in. Never has there been a word less elegant than the hideous American import that is 'playdate'; yet it has somehow become the accepted term for a certain type of joyful tea party, at which babies are plonked down in a circle on the floor, a few toys between them, and mothers are free to revel in the sordid delights of relived birthing nightmares. Once installed, effuse about the hostess's decisions on high chairs and sleeping arrangements, and pretend not to have noticed the adjacent creamy stain on the sofa or the lingering popcorn-ish odour in the upstairs corridor. A tip here for those still breastfeeding is to try not to ingest too much caffeine: although tempting, it will later be regretted when, come night-time, both jaw-clenching mother and baby are bouncing off the walls.

HOW TO PUSH A BUGGY IN SNOW

TO prepare for the adventure, first find a way to add some weight to the buggy in order to make it absolutely as stable as possible. Then, if there is not a wrist strap already, improvise one, using a belt or scarf tied between your body and the handlebars. Triple check that the baby is safely strapped in to the buggy, with all straps tightened and all loose items secured. Then ready, STEADY, go.

Be sure to walk very, very slowly and carefully. Avoid sudden movements. Hold the handlebars firmly (leather gloves will improve grip). Do not use the buggy to help one balance, since this has the potential to propel the wheels across the ice.

If the buggy starts to slide, steer *into* the slide (just as one should do when a car skids).

If faced with a steep slope, put added pressure on the buggy's handlebars in order to force the front wheels to become elevated. This ensures that the baby does not tip forwards but instead remains level. Walk with the knees bent, again very, very slowly, and at all costs avoid leaning forward, because this makes losing one's balance much more likely.

Alternatively, improvise a sledge, channel your inner Father Christmas, and ho! ho! ho! together all the way home.

LA LA LA

IT is a little known fact that it is the law in Britain that every baby must spend at least three minutes a day dancing in the kitchen. Hells bells, OK, it is not the law exactly, but it downright ought to be. For how better to set the tone for a joyful day ahead?

So, the playlist. Admit it: the main reason one wanted a baby in the first place is that it offers an excuse to play cheesy, totally uncool pop music at top volume as much as one wants. So *carpe diem*! The very concept of music designed especially for babies is to be shunned like the blight on society that it is. So beware, for instance, those ubiquitous CDs of the local music group's take on Beatles' songs: their purchase will be much regretted come a long drive to Cornwall when your baby's first word is 'Again!', 'Again!', 'Again!', piped up from the backseat of the car every three minutes. Introduce your baby to the real deal instead: *Abbey Road*, for example, which all of you can enjoy. Reggae is almost always a hit too, for some reason. Generally music is fantastic for the car, as opposed to toys, which just get chucked down the side of the car seat, cueing not only tears but also huge potential for accidents as you try to drive one-handed while groping blindly behind you to retrieve them.

Music can also be a useful element of the bedtime routine. Just be sure to choose something that you can face listening to over, and over, and over again. The baby does not mind, just as long as it is familiar. Beautiful balladeers range from Sufjan Stevens to The Carpenters, depending on taste. Also consider the duller end of the spectrum. For example, babies tend to love Norah Jones, a bit like the way they will happily sit for hours staring at a Damien Hirst dot painting. This is not necessarily a compliment, mind.

Alternatively, consider introducing classical music at an early age. Mozart, for example, is always a winner. Here are a few suggestions:

MOZART'S BEST FOR DANCING/DRUMMING/MARCHING

KV 384   *'Singt Dem Großen Bassa Lieder' from the opera* Die Entfuehrung aus dem Serail *(The Abduction from the Seraglio)*

KV 621   *Act 1, N.4 (Marcia) from the opera* La clemenza di Tito *(The Clemency of Titus)*

KV 214   *March in C*

KV 384   *'Bassa Selim Lebe Lange!' from the opera* Die Entfuehrung aus dem Serail

KV 249   *March in D*

KV 603   *Contredanses No. 1 in D Major*

KV 361   *Fourth movement (Menuetto) of Serenade No. 10 for thirteen wind instruments*

KV 603   *Contredanses No. 2 in B Flat Major*

MOZART'S BEST FOR SLEEPING/RELAXING/CALMING

KV 339   *Fifth movement (Laudate Dominum) of* Vesperae solennes de confessore

KV 622   *Second movement (Adagio) of Concerto in A for Clarinet*

KV 410   *Canonic Adagio in F Major for Two Bassett Horns and Bassoon*

KV 618   Ave verum corpus

KV 617   *Second movement of Adagio and Rondo in C for Flute, Oboe, Viola, Violoncello and Glass Harmonica*

(The letters KV refer to Koechel-Verzeichnis, the standard catalogue of Mozart's works.)

VACCINES

CONTROVERSIAL as vaccines are, here is a reference guide to what the British government recommends in the first year or so. Do it? Don't do it? Delay it? Whatever route you choose, do be mindful about how and where you do your research: there is a lot of misinformation out there in the wilds of the Internet.

When to immunize	Vaccine given	Diseases protected against
2 months old	DTaP/IPV/Hib + pneumococcal conjugate vaccine (PCV)	Diphtheria,* tetanus,[†] pertussis (whooping cough),[§] polio** and *Haemophilus influenzae* type B (Hib)[††]; pneumococcal infection[§§]
3 months old	DTaP/IPV/Hib + MenC	Diphtheria, tetanus, pertussis, polio and *Haemophilus influenzae* type B (Hib); meningitis C***
4 months old	DTaP/IPV/Hib + MenC + PCV	Diphtheria, tetanus, pertussis, polio and *Haemophilus influenzae* type B (Hib); meningitis C; pneumococcal infection
Around 12 months old	Hib/MenC	*Haemophilus influenza* type B (Hib); meningitis C
Around 13 months old	MMR[†††] + PCV	Measles, mumps and rubella; pneumococcal infection

Source: NHS

---

* First introduced in 1923.
[†] First introduced in 1926.
§ First introduced in 1914 (though in a different form, which killed the entire cell).
** First introduced in 1955.
[††] First introduced in 1992.
§§ First introduced in 1946.
*** First introduced in 1975 (though the current version did not become available until 1999).
[†††] First introduced in 1988.

HERE'S TO APATHY

APATHY: the secret to successful, sane mothering. Because while some of the problems that arise during the first year of a baby's life do require early intervention (for example, a baby who is able to fall asleep only when sucking eventually needs to be taught how to fall asleep another way – there is fundamentally no getting round it), a huge number of other problems can be solved by, quite simply, doing nothing. Left alone, they will fix themselves, as if by magic. Yes, it's true. Babies change so much from week to week that a fair amount of what they do turns out to be just a brief phase. Worrying about how to stop him wriggling around on the changing mat? How to stop him waking up crying every time his dummy falls out of his mouth? How to discourage him from biting the nipple? Just muddle through as best you can and amazingly often the problem will fix itself of its own accord in a mere matter of weeks, just by virtue of time passing – quickly to be replaced by a whole new set of challenges, of course.

This is a theory of childcare that can be applied throughout one's offspring's formative years. In the words of D.H. Lawrence, 'How to begin to educate a child. First rule, leave him alone. Second rule, leave him alone. Third rule, leave him alone. That is the whole beginning . . . Babies should invariably be taken away from their modern mothers and given, not to yearning and maternal old maids, but to rather stupid fat women who can't be bothered with them.' It is an approach that has recently re-emerged in a number of new incarnations: the Idle Parent (as coined by Tom Hodgkinson in *The Idler*), the Slack Dad (ditto Nicholas Lezard in the *Guardian*) and so on.

In summary, then, let us raise a glass to apathy! And with all that time saved by not trawling baby books for endless conflicting advice (most of which does not fit one's baby anyway, and even if it does one never has the energy to follow it), just think what one could achieve. Here are a few ideas:

1. Stare out the window at the clouds.
2. Write a diary of the first few weeks of motherhood. Just one sentence a day is plenty. Leave a notepad by the cot, maybe, or copy and paste emails written to update friends.
3. Have sex of some sort: alone, in company, whatever.
4. Plant herbs: mint, not marijuana. Study after study has shown that, whatever the country and whatever the culture, growing something is the one activity proved time and again to increase one's levels of happiness.
5. Paint your nails fluorescent pink, or some other inappropriately teenage shade.
6. Write to the Prime Minister to urge him to take immediate action to combat climate change: 10 Downing Street, London SW1A 2AA.
7. Learn to cut your own hair. You will save yourself a fortune.
8. Renovate your house. Though only if you want to be broke and angry for the next three years.
9. Dance to Madonna in the kitchen.
10. (Re)learn the periodic table, which systematizes all the elements that make up our world – yes, even your baby. And like the Tube map or Penguin books, it is an exceedingly aesthetically pleasing design. First published by Russian (Siberian, to be precise) chemist Dmitri Mendeleev in 1869, it has since been repeatedly adapted as new elements are discovered.

THE PERIODIC TABLE OF ELEMENTS

Key:

6	atomic number
Carbon	name of element
C	chemical number
12.01	atomic mass

Non-metals · Transition metals

IA Alkali metals	IIA Alkaline earth metals	IIIB	IVB	VB	VIB	VIIB	VIII	VIII	VIII	IB	IIB	IIIA	IVA	VA	VIA	VIIA	Noble gases
1 Hydrogen **H** 1.01																	2 Helium **He** 4.00
3 Lithium **Li** 6.94	4 Beryllium **Be** 9.01											5 Boron **B** 10.81	6 Carbon **C** 12.01	7 Nitrogen **N** 14.01	8 Oxygen **O** 16.00	9 Fluorine **F** 19.00	10 Neon **Ne** 20.18
11 Sodium **Na** 22.99	12 Magnesium **Mg** 24.31											13 Aluminium **Al** 26.98	14 Silicon **Si** 28.09	15 Phosphorus **P** 30.97	16 Sulphur **S** 32.07	17 Chlorine **Cl** 35.45	18 Argon **Ar** 39.95
19 Potassium **K** 39.10	20 Calcium **Ca** 40.08	21 Scandium **Sc** 44.96	22 Titanium **Ti** 47.88	23 Vanadium **V** 50.94	24 Chromium **Cr** 52.00	25 Manganese **Mn** 54.94	26 Iron **Fe** 55.85	27 Cobalt **Co** 58.93	28 Nickel **Ni** 58.69	29 Copper **Cu** 63.55	30 Zinc **Zn** 65.38	31 Gallium **Ga** 69.72	32 Germanium **Ge** 72.64	33 Arsenic **As** 74.92	34 Selenium **Se** 78.96	35 Bromine **Br** 79.904	36 Krypton **Kr** 83.80
37 Rubidium **Rb** 85.47	38 Strontium **Sr** 87.62	39 Yttrium **Y** 88.91	40 Zirconium **Zr** 91.22	41 Niobium **Nb** 92.91	42 Molybdenum **Mo** 95.96	43 Technetium **Tc** 97.91	44 Ruthenium **Ru** 101.07	45 Rhodium **Rh** 102.91	46 Palladium **Pd** 106.42	47 Silver **Ag** 107.87	48 Cadmium **Cd** 112.41	49 Indium **In** 114.82	50 Tin **Sn** 118.71	51 Antimony **Sb** 121.76	52 Tellurium **Te** 127.60	53 Iodine **I** 126.9045	54 Xenon **Xe** 131.29
55 Caesium **Cs** 132.91	56 Barium **Ba** 137.33	57 Lanthanum **La** 138.91 (see below)	72 Hafnium **Hf** 178.49	73 Tantalum **Ta** 180.94	74 Tungsten **W** 183.85	75 Rhenium **Re** 186.21	76 Osmium **Os** 190.23	77 Iridium **Ir** 192.22	78 Platinum **Pt** 195.08	79 Gold **Au** 196.97	80 Mercury **Hg** 200.59	81 Thallium **Tl** 204.38	82 Lead **Pb** 207.2	83 Bismuth **Bi** 208.98	84 Polonium **Po** 209	85 Astatine **At** 210	86 Radon **Rn** 222
87 Francium **Fr** 223	88 Radium **Ra** 226	89 Actinium **Ac** 227 (see below)	104 Rutherfordium **Rf** 261	105 Dubnium **Db** 262	106 Seaborgium **Sg** 266	107 Bohrium **Bh** 264	108 Hassium **Hs** 277	109 Meitnerium **Mt** 268	110 Darmstadtium **Ds** 271	111 Roentgenium **Rg** 272	112 Copernicum **Cn** 285						

Rare earth elements — Lanthanide series

Lanthanide series	58 Cerium **Ce** 140.12	59 Praseodymium **Pr** 140.91	60 Neodymium **Nd** 144.24	61 Promethium **Pm** 145	62 Samarium **Sm** 150.36	63 Europium **Eu** 151.96	64 Gadolinium **Gd** 157.25	65 Terbium **Tb** 158.93	66 Dysprosium **Dy** 162.50	67 Holmium **Ho** 164.93	68 Erbium **Er** 167.26	69 Thulium **Tm** 168.93	70 Ytterbium **Yb** 173.05	71 Lutetium **Lu** 174.97
Actinide series	90 Thorium **Th** 232.04	91 Protactinium **Pa** 231.04	92 Uranium **U** 238.03	93 Neptunium **Np** 237	94 Plutonium **Pu** 244	95 Americium **Am** 243	96 Curium **Cm** 247	97 Berkelium **Bk** 247	98 Californium **Cf** 251	99 Einsteinium **Es** 252	100 Fermium **Fm** 257	101 Mendelevium **Md** 258	102 Nobelium **No** 259	103 Lawrencium **Lr** 262

Tc Technetium: The first element to be produced artificially.

Hf Hafnium: Named after Hafinia, the Latin name for Copenhagen.

H Hydrogen: The most abundant element in the universe.

'SING A SONG OF SIXPENCE', AND SO ON

ALONG with what labour contractions feel like and how to care for a baby's penis, the words to nursery rhymes are another aspect of motherhood that one is just magically supposed to know. Yet in most cases one doesn't, especially these days, when many of us have hardly even *seen* a baby until we have our own, let alone had to entertain such a tiny tot. So here are the complete texts of some of the best nursery rhymes for those under twelve months. After all, one doesn't want to embarrass oneself at one's first Mummy and Me group, does one?

SING A SONG OF SIXPENCE

Sing a song of sixpence,
A pocket full of rye.
Four and twenty blackbirds,
Baked in a pie.

When the pie was opened,
The birds began to sing;
Wasn't that a dainty dish,
To set before the king?

The king was in his counting house,
Counting out his money;
The queen was in the parlour,
Eating bread and honey.*

---

* This third verse appears as a recurring motif in Virginia Woolf's final

The maid was in the garden,
Hanging out the clothes;
When down came a blackbird
And pecked off her nose.

BAA, BAA, BLACK SHEEP

Baa, baa, black sheep,
Have you any wool?
Yes sir, yes sir,
Three bags full.
One for the master,
One for the dame,
And one for the little boy
Who lives down the lane.*

POP GOES THE WEASEL

Half a pound of tuppenny rice,
Half a pound of treacle.
That's the way the money goes,
Pop! goes the weasel.

---

novel, *Between the Acts*, which was first published in 1941 a few months after her death. The words are heard on a gramophone that plays in the background as a group of English villagers prepare for a local pageant they are staging, possibly as a comment on the traditional roles into which men and women so often fall.

* Manchester, 1951: 'Baa, Baa, Black Sheep' became the first song ever to be digitally recorded and played on a computer. The computer in question was a Ferranti Mark 1, which was the world's first commercially available computer.

Every night when I get home
The monkey's on the table,
Take a stick and knock it off,
Pop! goes the weasel.*

ONE, TWO, THREE, FOUR, FIVE

One, two, three, four, five,
Once I caught a fish alive,
Six, seven, eight, nine, ten,
Then I let it go again.

Why did you let it go?
Because it bit my finger so.
Which finger did it bite?
This little finger on my right.

POLLY PUT THE KETTLE ON

Polly put the kettle on,
Polly put the kettle on,
Polly put the kettle on,
We'll all have tea.

Sukey take it off again,
Sukey take it off again,
Sukey take it off again,
They've all gone away.†

---

* A version of 'Pop Goes The Weasel' by Anthony Newley reached number twelve in the charts in 1961.
† In *Barnaby Rudge* by Charles Dickens (1841), a raven named Grip squawks

THE GRAND OLD DUKE OF YORK*

The grand old Duke of York,
He had ten thousand men;
He marched them up to the top of the hill,
And he marched them down again.

And when they were up, they were up,
And when they were down, they were down,
And when they were only half way up,
They were neither up nor down.

HERE WE GO ROUND THE MULBERRY BUSH

Here we go round the mulberry bush,
The mulberry bush,
The mulberry bush.
Here we go round the mulberry bush
On a cold and frosty morning.†

---

the words 'Polly, put the kettle on. Hurrah! Polly, put the kettle on and we'll all have tea. Grip, Grip, Grip-Grip the Clever, Grip the Wicked, Grip the Knowing.' It was the first time the rhyme had appeared in print.
* Said 'Grand Old Duke of York' is most commonly thought to be Frederick, Duke of York and Albany (1763–1827), who was George III's second son and Commander-in-Chief of the British army during the Napoleonic Wars.
† A mulberry is a member of the *Moraceae* family of plants, which are native to Asia. Species vary in appearance, but most look a bit like a blackberry or a raspberry. The most common are the black mulberry, the red mulberry and the white mulberry. They do not, however, grow on bushes, but on trees.

HUMPTY DUMPTY*

Humpty Dumpty sat on a wall,
Humpty Dumpty had a great fall.
All the king's horses and all the king's men
Couldn't put Humpty together again.

---

* 'Don't stand chattering to yourself like that,' Humpty Dumpty said, looking at [Alice] for the first time, 'but tell me your name and your business.'

'My name is Alice, but—'

'It's a stupid name enough!' Humpty Dumpty interrupted impatiently. 'What does it mean?'

'Must a name mean something?' Alice asked doubtfully.

'Of course it must,' Humpty Dumpty said with a short laugh: 'my name means the shape I am — and a good handsome shape it is, too. With a name like yours, you might be any shape, almost.'

'Why do you sit out here all alone?' said Alice, not wishing to begin an argument.

'Why, because there's nobody with me!' cried Humpty Dumpty. 'Did you think I didn't know the answer to that? Ask another.'

'Don't you think you'd be safer down on the ground?' Alice went on, not with any idea of making another riddle, but simply in her good-natured anxiety for the queer creature. 'That wall is so very narrow!'

'What tremendously easy riddles you ask!' Humpty Dumpty growled out. 'Of course I don't think so! Why, if ever I did fall off — which there's no chance of — but if I did—' Here he pursed up his lips, and looked so solemn and grand that Alice could hardly help laughing. 'If I did fall,' he went on, 'the King has promised me — ah, you may turn pale, if you like! You didn't think I was going to say that, did you? The King has promised me — with his very own mouth — to — to—'

'To send all his horses and all his men,' Alice interrupted, rather unwisely.

'Now I declare that's too bad!' Humpty Dumpty cried, breaking into a sudden passion. 'You've been listening at doors — and behind trees — and down chimneys — or you couldn't have known it!'

'I haven't indeed!' Alice said very gently. 'It's in a book.'

'Ah, well! They may write such things in a book,' Humpty Dumpty said in a calmer tone. 'That's what you call a History of England, that is. Now, take a good look at me! I'm one that has spoken to a King, I am: mayhap you'll never see such another: and, to show you I'm not proud, you may shake hands with me!' And he grinned almost from ear to ear, as he leant forwards (and as nearly as possible fell off the wall in doing so) and offered Alice his hand. She watched him a little anxiously as she took it. 'If he smiled much more the ends of his mouth might meet behind,' she thought: 'And then I don't know what would happen to his head! I'm afraid it would come off!'

Lewis Carroll, Alice Through the Looking Glass (1871)

LONDON BRIDGE

London Bridge is falling down,
Falling down, falling down.
London Bridge is falling down,
My fair lady.

Build it up with wood and clay,
Wood and clay, wood and clay,
Build it up with wood and clay,
My fair lady.

Wood and clay will wash away,
Wash away, wash away,
Wood and clay will wash away,
My fair lady.

Build it up with bricks and mortar,
Bricks and mortar, bricks and
    mortar,
Build it up with bricks and mortar,
My fair lady.

Bricks and mortar will not stay,
Will not stay, will not stay,
Bricks and mortar will not stay,
My fair lady.

Build it up with iron and steel,
Iron and steel, iron and steel,
Build it up with iron and steel,
My fair lady.

Iron and steel will bend and bow,
Bend and bow, bend and bow,
Iron and steel will bend and bow,
My fair lady.

Build it up with silver and gold,
Silver and gold, silver and gold,
Build it up with silver and gold,
My fair lady.

Silver and gold will be stolen away,
Stolen away, stolen away,
Silver and gold will be stolen away,
My fair lady.

Set a man to watch all night,
Watch all night, watch all night,
Set a man to watch all night,
My fair lady.

Suppose the man should fall asleep,
Fall asleep, fall asleep,
Suppose the man should fall asleep?
My fair lady.

Give him a pipe to smoke all night,
Smoke all night, smoke all night,
Give him a pipe to smoke all night,
My fair lady.

TWINKLE, TWINKLE, LITTLE STAR

Twinkle, twinkle, little star,
How I wonder what you are!
Up above the world so high,
Like a diamond in the sky!
Twinkle, twinkle, little star,
How I wonder what you are!

When the blazing sun is gone,
When he nothing shines upon,
Then you show your little light,
Twinkle, twinkle, all the night.
Twinkle, twinkle, little star,
How I wonder what you are!

Then the traveller in the dark,
Thanks you for your tiny spark,
He could not see which way to go,

If you did not twinkle so.
Twinkle, twinkle, little star,
How I wonder what you are!

In the dark blue sky you keep,
And often through my curtains
    peep,
For you never shut your eye,
Twinkle, twinkle, little star,
How I wonder what you are!

As your bright and tiny spark,
Lights the traveller in the dark,
Though I know not what you are,
Twinkle, twinkle, little star.
Twinkle, twinkle, little star,
How I wonder what you are!*

---

* 'Twinkle, Twinkle, Little Star' was written in 1806 by Jane Taylor, a twenty-three-year-old living in Lavenham in Suffolk, and first published in a collection of poems called *Rhymes for the Nursery* (1806), written by her and her older sister Ann. In a letter to another writer friend whom she had just been to visit, written just before she composed her most famous lines, Jane expressed her excitement that her parents (with whom she still lived, since she was unmarried) had allowed her a Room of her Own:

> My verses have certainly one advantage to boast, beyond any that ever before escaped from my pen;— that of being composed in my own study . . . one of my first engagements on my return home, was to fit up an unoccupied attic, hitherto devoted only to household lumber: this I removed by the most spirited exertions, and supplied its place with all the apparatus necessary for a poet; which, you know, is not of a very extensive nature:—a few book-shelves, a table for my writing-desk, one chair for myself, and another for my muse, is a pretty accurate inventory of my furniture. But though my study cannot boast the elegance of yours, it possesses one advantage which, as a poet, you ought to allow surpasses them all— it commands a view of the country;— the only room in the house, except one, which is thus favored; and to me this is invaluable. You may now expect me to do wonders.

Taylor later died of breast cancer at the age of just forty.

TEDDY BEAR'S PICNIC

If you go down in the woods today
You're sure of a big surprise.
If you go down in the woods today
You'd better go in disguise.

For ev'ry bear that ever there was
Will gather there for certain, because
Today's the day the teddy bears have their picnic.

LITTLE MISS MUFFET

Little Miss Muffet
Sat on a tuffet,
Eating her curds and whey;
Along came a spider,
Who sat down beside her
And frightened Miss Muffet away.

THREE BLIND MICE

Three blind mice. Three blind mice.
See how they run. See how they run.
They all ran after the farmer's wife,
Who cut off their tails with a carving knife,
Did you ever see such a thing in your life,
As three blind mice?

ORANGES AND LEMONS

Oranges and lemons,
Say the bells of St Clement's.
You owe me five farthings,
Say the bells of St Martin's.
When will you pay me?
Say the bells of Old Bailey.
When I grow rich,
Say the bells of Shoreditch.
When will that be?
Say the bells of Stepney.
I do not know,
Says the great bell of Bow.

RING A-RING O' ROSES

Ring a-ring o' roses,
A pocketful of posies.
A-tishoo!, A-tishoo!
We all fall down.*

---

* According to the *Oxford Dictionary of Nursery Rhymes*, it is rarely true that a nursery rhyme is based directly on an historical event. Take 'Ring A-Ring O' Roses', for example. Trivia enthusiasts commonly claim that it refers to the Great Plague of 1665 – despite the fact that a rosy rash was not a symptom, posies were not carried as protection, and contemporary accounts do not mention sneezing as the final fatal symptom. Furthermore, a version of it exists in a number of cultures, suggesting that it dates to well before the seventeenth century. So unfortunately that is one less piece of information with which to bore the other mothers at the park.

TEETHING

'ADAM and Eve had many advantages, but the principal one was that they escaped teething.' So mused Mark Twain in his 1894 novel *Pudd'nhead Wilson*. He goes on to describe the way a teething baby will sometimes

> let go scream after scream and squall after squall, then climax the thing with 'holding his breath' — that frightful specialty of the teething nursling, in the throes of which the creature exhausts its lungs, then is convulsed with noiseless squirmings and twistings and kickings in the effort to get its breath, while the lips turn blue and the mouth stands wide and rigid, offering for inspection one wee tooth set in the lower rim of a hoop of red gums; and when the appalling stillness has endured until one is sure the lost breath will never return, a nurse comes flying, and dashes water in the child's face, and — presto! the lungs fill, and instantly discharge a shriek, or a yell, or a howl which bursts the listening ear and surprises the owner of it into saying words which would not go well with a halo if he had one.

Teething will indeed dominate much of a baby's first year. Pump your baby with drugs if that's your bag, try homeopathic tablets or amber necklaces, or just offer lots of hugs and brace yourself for some sleepless nights. Also key is to stumble across some distraction or other that never fails: a tinkling music box or a revolving night light, for instance, will help keep both of you just that little bit calmer throughout the midnight hours.

Upper baby teeth:

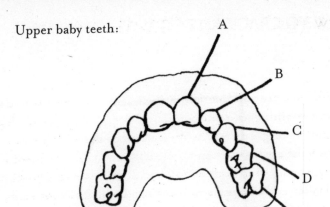

Lower baby teeth:

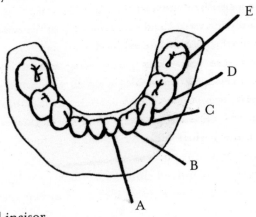

A. Central incisor
B. Lateral incisor
C. Canine tooth
D. First molar
E. Second molar

HOW TO CRACK AN EGG WITH ONE HAND

BECAUSE, once you have a baby, you have to learn how to do almost everything with one hand.

Hold the egg with whichever hand you use to write with. Position the egg so that your thumb and first finger are holding the bigger end, while your middle and third fingers are holding the smaller end and pressing it against the heel of your palm.

Tap the egg sharply and firmly on a flat surface such as the kitchen counter — *not* on the side of a bowl. The point of impact should be between your thumb and first finger and the rest of your fingers. The aim is not to smash the egg but merely to create a smallish crack in the shell. To help with this, be sure to keep your wrist dead straight, which will prevent the shell from cracking in multiple places.

Next, use your thumb and your middle finger to apply gentle pressure to both sides of the egg, and then — keeping the pressure even on each side — to slide the shell in opposite directions. The two halves will separate cleanly and the egg yolk and egg white will fall into the bowl below.

Then await the applause.

THE ART OF CHINESE

EVERY child born in the twenty-first century is most definitely going to need to know how to write his or her name in Chinese. It's the future, et cetera. So, here's a guide for the UK's top five most popular boys' and girls' names.

Jack	澤渥
Oliver	軻俐發
Thomas	鎧宓士
Harry	夏禮
Joshua	俎恕埡
Olivia	婀莉斐埡
Ruby	璐毖
Emily	藝妙莉
Grace	潔麗絲
Jessica	謝絲佧

BABY FOOD

BY the time a baby is four months old, 51 per cent of mothers will have introduced solid food. This figure rises to 82 per cent by five months and 99 per cent by six months, according to the NHS's most recent Infant Feeding Survey. The real question, however, is what *sort* of solid food. The first ready-made offerings were launched in 1867 by Henri Nestlé, and swiftly followed by a flurry of imitators. In 1902, Ada Ballin, in her best-selling manual *From Cradle to School: A Book for Mothers*, suggested that mothers match the type of food they feed their baby to the baby's personality: dull dishes of eggs and vegetables for the high-spirited child, stimulating cups of coffee for breakfast and wine for supper for the milder-mannered munchkin. This theory no longer holds sway, unsurprisingly, but we remain swamped with options, as well as with books about how to make our own delicate mushes. Most of these books are, however, a bit of a con, since the technique really is not rocket science. Steam a fruit or a vegetable, whiz it into a purée with a hand blender, and then serve or freeze. Stranded without a hand blender? Say, on a spaceship or inside an igloo? No problem — just use a fork to mash up a banana or an avocado, both near-perfect foods.

NUTRITIONAL CONTENT OF ONE MEDIUM-SIZED BANANA AND ONE MEDIUM-SIZED AVOCADO

Vitamins

	Banana	Avocado
Vitamin A	75.5 IU	293 IU
Vitamin C	10.3mg	20.1mg
Vitamin D	–	–
Vitamin E	0.1mg	4.2mg
Vitamin K	0.6mcg	42.2mcg
Thiamin	0.1mg	0.1mg
Riboflavin	0.1mg	0.3mg
Niacin	0.8mg	3.5mg
Vitamin B6	0.4mg	0.5mg
Folate	23.6mcg	163mcg
Pantothenic acid	0.4mg	2.8mg
Choline	11.6mg	28.5mg
Betaine	0.1mg	1.4mg

Minerals

	Banana	Avocado
Calcium	5.9mg	24.1mg
Iron	0.3mg	1.1mg
Magnesium	31.9mg	58.3mg
Phosphorus	26mg	105mg
Potassium	422mg	975mg
Sodium	1.2mg	14.1mg
Zinc	0.2mg	1.3mg
Copper	0.1mg	0.4mg
Manganese	0.3mg	0.3mg
Selenium	1.2mcg	0.8mcg
Fluoride	2.6mcg	14.1mcg

Alternatively, acquaint yourself with Baby-Led Weaning, the gist of which is as follows. The classic technique of feeding a baby by shovelling spoonfuls of puréed food into his or her mouth is a throwback to a generation ago, when it was commonplace to start solids at three months. But recent research has found that six months is a far more appropriate age, by which time babies are entirely capable not only of feeding themselves, rather than being harassed by a bothersome spoon just as they are having a profound thought about a rattle, but also of eating the very same food that you eat, only without the salt/sugar/nuts/honey/chilli (plus a few other exceptions). In other words, Baby-Led Weaning is the lazy person's option, huzzah! For more information, look up the website or books of Gill Rapley, the foremost expert on the subject.

In some ways, solids are a boon. A piece of toast keeps a six-month-old baby happy for longer than even the spangliest of toys, and all of a sudden it is actually possible to sit at the kitchen table drinking tea having lovely long phone conversations with your friends while the baby sits in the high chair merrily gnawing away. At the same time, however, solids are an awful hassle: at the end of each meal, it is as though you, your baby and your kitchen floor have all been machine-gunned with food. But do not despair as you find yourself on your hands and knees scrubbing away at some squashed, cold broccoli for what seems like the hundredth time that day. Instead, be inspired by the approach taken in *The Home-Maker* by Dorothy Canfield Fisher (1924) : 'The attic was piled to the eaves with old newspapers. Every day [the children] Helen or Henry brings down a fresh supply. We spread them around two or three thick, drop our grease on them with all the peace of mind in the world, whisk them up at night . . . and have a spotless floor . . . [it] is an original exercise of the human intelligence in contact with real life.' Also consider making the experience a little less depressing by buying yourself a fabulous pinny. Though with the mess most babies make, a pinny may not be sufficient: what you really need is a hijab. Which raises the question, why doesn't Cath Kidston make hijabs? They'd be a best-seller. Let's write to her.

A FEW WORDS OF WISDOM

There never was a child so lovely but his mother was glad to get him asleep.

Ralph Waldo Emerson (1803–82)

All women become like their mothers. That is their tragedy. No man does. That's his.

Oscar Wilde (1854–1900)

A mother is not a person to lean on, but a person to make leaning unnecessary.

Dorothy Canfield Fisher (1879–1958)

Whatever else is unsure in this stinking dunghill of a world a mother's love is not.

James Joyce (1882–1941)

Your children are not your children.
They are the sons and daughters of Life's longing for itself.
They come through you but not from you,
And though they are with you, yet they belong not to you.

You may give them your love but not your thoughts.

For they have their own thoughts.

You may house their bodies but not their souls,

For their souls dwell in the house of tomorrow, which you

cannot visit, not even in your dreams.

You may strive to be like them, but seek not to make them like you.

For life goes not backward nor tarries with yesterday.

You are the bows from which your children as living arrows are

sent forth.

Khalil Gibran (1883–1931)

At work, you think of the children you have left at home. At home, you think of the work you've left unfinished. Such a struggle is unleashed within yourself. Your heart is rent.

Golda Meir (1898–1978)

Death and taxes and childbirth! There's never any convenient time for any of them!

Margaret Mitchell (1900–49)

Why do grandparents and grandchildren get along so well? They have the same enemy: the mother.

Claudette Colbert (1903–96)

If you've never been hated by your child, you've never been a parent.

Bette Davis (1908–89)

Now the thing about having a baby — and I can't be the first person to have noticed this — is that thereafter you have it.

Jean Kerr (1922–2003)

If you bungle raising your children, I don't think whatever else you do well matters very much.

Jacqueline Kennedy Onassis (1929–94)

When you are a mother, you are never really alone in your thoughts. A mother always has to think twice, once for herself and once for her child.

Sophia Loren (1934–)

TALLY-HO, YOU'RE OFF

HAVE no illusions: going on holiday with a baby is not a holiday, it is just childcare in a different setting. But if what they say is true, that a change is as good as a rest, then it is still worth it. For though it might seem like an immense hassle at the time, in retrospect one is almost always pleased one made the effort, instead of just standing on the sidelines, sippy cup in hand, watching life pass one by. Anyway, going on holiday with a baby is easy-peasy-lemon-squeezy compared to going on holiday with a toddler, so make the most of it. Invest in a travel cot and some fun CDs (see page 160) and tally-ho, you're off.

Flying, however, is for fools. Not only and most importantly is it ecological suicide, but on a more immediate level it also requires that one faff around obtaining the baby a passport, which is never fun: you try getting a baby to hold its head up long enough to have a passport photo taken — you are guaranteed to regret it (though if you *must* get a passport, here is a tip: lie the baby down on a white sheet, take the photo yourself and then email it in to a website that specializes in developing passport photos). So take the train. Or, alternatively, drive. That way, one is subject to nobody's timetable but the baby's: stop the car, have a picnic, change a nappy, look at the view, bemoan the weather and so on. Although it must be admitted that it will help *a lot* if your baby is close friends with his or her dummy.

These, according to the AA, are Britain's ten most scenic drives.

1. Exmoor and the sea: steep coastline, stone villages, empty moorland

Route: Lynton–Malmsmead–Porlock–Luccombe–Minehead–Watchet–Elworthy–Winsford–Simonsbath–South Molton–Great Torrington–Bideford–Barnstaple–Arlington–Blackmoor Gate–Lynton.

2. Hills of West Wessex: Salisbury Cathedral, Stonehenge, valleys and rugged hills

Route: Salisbury–Old Sarum–Stonehenge–Warminster–Frome–Wells–Cheddar–Glastonbury–Bruton–Stourhead–Shaftesbury–Fonthill Bishop–Wilton–Salisbury.

3. Journey across the Weald: along the edge of the North Downs and through the orchards of the 'Garden of England'

Route: Penshurst–Hever–Limpsfield–Sevenoaks–Ightham–Mereworth–Paddock Wood–Lamberhurst–Cranbrook–Tenterden–Northiam–Bodiam–Burwash–Cross-in-hand–Rotherfield–Tunbridge Wells.

4. The Downs of Hampshire: lush valleys and panoramic views of where battle fleets throughout history have set sail

Route: Winchester–Stockbridge–Danebury Hillfort–Nether Wallop–Houghton–Mottisfont–Romsey–Ampfield–Otterbourne–Bishop's Waltham–Portsdown Hill–Purbrook–Hambledon–West Meon–New Alresford–Winchester.

5. Castles on Welsh marches: testaments to a turbulent age when the Normans fought the Welsh

Route: Chepstow–Monmouth–Symonds Yat–Goodrich–Ross-on-Wye–Skenfrith–Grosmont–Hay-on-Wye–Bronllys–Brecon–Pontsticill–Talybont-on-Usk–Abergavenny–Raglan–Usk–Caerleon–Penhow–Chepstow.

6. Pembroke Coast National Park: heritage coastline, fine castles and the village that inspired Dylan Thomas to write Under Milk Wood

Route: Manorbier–Pembroke–Haverfordwest–St David's–Mathry–Fishguard–Newport–Molygrove–Cardigan–Dre-fach and Felindre–Carmarthen–Laugharne–Tenby–Manorbier.

7. Shropshire and the Severn valley: stunning scenery and the birthplace of the industrial revolution

Route: Shrewsbury–Acton Burnell–Church Stretton–Craven Arms–Ludlow–Cleehill–Bewdley–Bridgnorth–Shipton–Much Wenlock–Ironbridge–Wroxeter–Shrewsbury.

8. Lakeland: Carlisle, the Lake District, Brougham Castle and Hadrian's Wall

Route: Carlisle–Caldbeck–Bassenthwaite–Whinlater Pass–Low Lorton–Buttermere–Keswick–Grasmere–Coniston–Hawkshead–Windermere–Patterdale–Penrith–Haltwhistle–Carlisle.

9. North Yorkshire from vale to moor: scenic villages, ancient abbeys and the wild openness of the moors

Route: York–Malton–Pickering–Goathland–Grosmont–Lealholm–Danby–Rosedale Abbey–Hutton-le-Hole–Gillamoor–Kirkbymoorside–Helmsley–Rievaulx Abbey–Kilburn White Horse–Coxwold–Wass–Sutton-on-the-Forest–York.

10. Highland Scotland: from the shores of Loch Ness to the west-coast fishing communities of Wester Ross

Route: Inverness–Drumnadrochit–Invermoriston–Dundreggan–Eilean Donan Castle–Stromeferry–Strathcarron Station–Lochcarron–Applecross–Fearnmore–Shieldaig–Torridon–Gairloch–Inverewe Garden–Gruinard Bay–Ardessie–Garve–Contin–Strathpeffer–Moniack Castle–Reelig Glen–Inverness.

Source: AA

Also consider Cornwall. Start at Portreath on the north coast and then head west, travelling around the Cornish peninsula all the way to Falmouth, a lovely Georgian town with fantastic fish and chips. The drive is about 100 miles in total. This route also offers an excuse to stay at Tresanton, one of the world's most beautiful, but also most expensive, hotels. For those of us who happen not to work at Goldman

Sachs, there are a number of charming B&Bs in the area too.

Some babies detest their car seat. If yours is one of them, and if s/he is lucky enough to have grandparents who are helpful (and not all are — never assume), an alternative option is simply to drive to the hotel nearest your house and hunker down there for the night, *sans* baby. For although you are highly likely to weep the entire way there, it is amazing what a long bath, some unbroken sleep and breakfast in bed can do for a weary mother's soul.

THE MANY WONDERS OF A WOODEN SPOON

Behold the child, by Nature's kindly law
Pleased with a rattle, tickled with a straw.

Alexander Pope, *An Essay on Man*, Epistle II (1722)

IN the short term, babies love all those hi-tech plastic monstrosities like baby swings or, when they are a few months older, baby bouncers. And admittedly they fulfil a function, which is to allow the new mother ten minutes of freedom to have a shower. However — and it is a huge however — so ugly are they that they cause some of us physically to recoil in horror at the very sight of them in our sitting room, which they will dominate with fascist aplomb. There is an obvious solution to this: don't buy any, and don't have showers. Most babies get bored with this sort of paraphernalia pretty quickly anyway. In the long term, there is far more play and pleasure to be had out of the old clichés of a wooden spoon and some tissue paper. Here are some other ideas of how to make your own baby toys:

- An old vitamin box filled with beans or rice works very well as a rattle.
- Fashion a trumpet out of a kitchen roll.
- Make a drum out of an old ice-cream pot, along with a wooden spoon for a drumstick.
- Remove the label of an old water bottle, refill it with water, and then add any of the following: drops of olive oil, tiny pieces of tin foil, a sprinkling of glitter. Securely glue or tape the bottle's lid back on, and then demonstrate the wonders of what happens when you hold it up to the sunshine and shake, shake, shake it. Marvellous.
- Wash out some old milk cartons, tape the tops down so they are flat, and bingo! — oversized building blocks just perfect for knocking down over and over and over again. Stuffing them with old newspaper will make them that bit sturdier, by the way.
- Stuff a sock full of tissue paper, and then tie a knot in the top. The crinkly sound it makes when held and squished by tiny hands will be music to your baby's ears.

PRIME MINISTERS

'SLEEP and a sense of history': this, according to Harold Wilson, is what it takes to be a successful prime minister. The same goes for being a successful mother. Keeping hold of the fact that the struggles that arise on a daily basis (how to get the baby to sleep, how to get the baby to eat, a spit-up stain on one's new dress) are ones with which women have grappled for many hundreds of years is essential to maintaining one's sense of proportion about the latest dose of drama. Here, then, is a list of all Britain's prime ministers — not solely as a reminder that one is still able to retain some real information, but also to recite to the baby while changing his or her nappy. It is amazing the laugh that can be elicited simply by proclaiming 'Disraeli' in an exaggerated fashion.

Name	Period of office	Political party
Sir Robert Walpole*	1721–42	Whig
Spencer Compton, Earl of Wilmington†	1742–3	Whig
Henry Pelham	1743–54	Whig
Thomas Pelham-Holles, Duke of Newcastle	1754–6 and 1757–62	Whig
William Cavendish, Duke of Devonshire	1756–7	Whig
John Stuart, Earl of Bute	1762–3	Tory
George Grenville	1763–5	Whig
Charles Wentworth, Marquess of Rockingham	1765–6 and 1782	Whig

* Walpole holds the record for the longest time spent in office: 20 years, 314 days.
† The Earl of Wilmington's tenure was followed by the longest gap ever between prime ministers: there were fifty-six days between his death and the appointment of Henry Pelham, when essentially nobody was in charge.

Name	Period of office	Political party
William Pitt 'the Elder', Earl of Chatham	1766–8	Whig
Augustus Henry Fitzroy, Duke of Grafton	1768–70	Whig
Lord North	1770–82	Tory
William Petty, Earl of Shelburne	1782–3	Whig
William Bentinck, Duke of Portland*	1783 and 1807–9	Whig
William Pitt 'the Younger'	1783–1801 and 1804–6	Tory
Henry Addington	1801–4	Tory
William Wyndham Grenville, Lord Grenville	1806–7	Whig
Spencer Perceval	1809–12	Tory
Robert Banks Jenkinson, Earl of Liverpool	1812–27	Tory
George Canning†	1827	Tory
Frederick Robinson, Viscount Goderich	1827–8	Tory
Arthur Wellesley, Duke of Wellington	1828–30	Tory
Earl Grey§	1830–34	Whig
William Lamb, Viscount Melbourne	1834 and 1835–41	Whig
Sir Robert Peel	1834–5 and 1841–6	Tory
Earl Russell	1846–51 and 1865–6	Liberal
The Earl of Derby	1852, 1858–9 and 1866–8	Conservative
The Earl of Aberdeen	1852–5	Tory
Viscount Palmerston	1855–8 and 1859–65	Liberal
Benjamin Disraeli	1868 and 1874–80	Conservative
William Ewart Gladstone	1868–74, 1880–85, 1886 and 1892–14	Liberal

* Portland's gardener, William Speechly, wrote the eighteenth century's foremost tome on the subject of how to grow a pineapple, *A Treatise on the Culture of the Pineapple* (1779).

† Holds the record for the shortest stint in office – just 199 days.

§ Had seventeen children (one of them illegitimately with Georgiana, Duchess of Devonshire), more than any other PM. He also had a rather delicious type of tea named after him.

Name	Period of office	Political party
Robert Gascoyne-Cecil, Marquess of Salisbury	1885–6, 1886–92 and 1895–1902	Conservative
The Earl of Rosebery	1894–5	Liberal
Arthur James Balfour	1902–5	Conservative
Henry Campbell-Bannerman	1905–8	Liberal
Herbert Henry Asquith	1908–16	Liberal
David Lloyd George	1916–22	Liberal
Andrew Bonar Law	1922–3	Conservative
Stanley Baldwin	1923, 1924–9, 1935–7	Conservative
James Ramsay MacDonald	1924 and 1929–35	Labour
Arthur Neville Chamberlain	1937–40	Conservative
Sir Winston Leonard Spencer Churchill*	1940–45 and 1951–55	Conservative
Clement Richard Attlee	1945–51	Labour
Anthony Eden	1955–7	Conservative
Harold Macmillan	1957–63	Conservative
Sir Alec Douglas-Home	1963–4	Conservative
Harold Wilson	1964–70 and 1974–6	Labour
Edward Heath	1970–74	Conservative
James Callaghan	1976–9	Labour
Margaret Thatcher	1979–90	Conservative
John Major	1990–97	Conservative
Tony Blair	1997–2007	Labour
Gordon Brown	2007–10	Labour
David Cameron	2010–present	Conservative

* Born on 30 November 1874, not (as commonly thought) in the loo at Blenheim Palace during a dance, but instead, as his father later wrote in a letter to his mother-in-law:

[Churchill's mother, Jennie] had a fall on Tuesday walking with the shooters, and a rather imprudent and rough drive in a pony carriage brought on the pains on Saturday night. We tried to stop them, but it was no use. They went on all Sunday. Of course the Oxford physician did not come. We telegraphed for the London man, Dr Hope, but he did not arrive till this morning. The country doctor is however a clever man, and the baby was safely born at 1.30 this morning after about 8 hrs labour.

SIX MONTHS OLD

IT is unwise to generalize about a baby at six months: some can crawl and some can't, some can speak Greek and some can't. The truth is, *babies develop at different rates. Get over it.* With this in mind, let us gaily sweep all our baby books off the shelf and go home. Or, alternatively, let us strive to stay specific and focus instead upon just one particular six-month-old: novelist Elizabeth Gaskell's daughter, Marianne.

March 10th Tuesday evening. 1835.

. . . Marianne is now becoming every day more interesting. She looks at and tries to take hold of everything. She has pretty good ideas of distance and does not try to catch sunbeams now, as she did two months ago. Her sense of sight is much improved lately in seeing objects at a distance, and distinguishing them. For instance I had her in my arms today in the drawing room, and her Papa was going out of the gate, and she evidently knew him; smiled and kicked. She begins to show a decided preference to those she likes; she puts out her little arms to come to me, and would I am sure, do so to her Papa. She catches the expression of a countenance to which she is accustomed directly; when we laugh, she laughs; and when I look attentive to William's reading, it is quite ridiculous to see her little face of gravity, and earnestness, as if she understood every word. I try always to let her look at anything which attracts her notice as long as she will, and when I see her looking intently at anything, I take her to it, and let her exercise all her senses upon it — even to tasting, if I am sure it can do her no harm. My object is to give her a habit of fixing her attention.

She takes great delight in motion just at present; dancing, jumping, shutting and opening the hand pleases her very much. I had no idea children at her age, made such continued noises; she shouts, and murmurs, and talks in her way, just like conversation, varying her tones &c. I wish we could know what is passing in her little mind. She likes anything like singing, but seems afraid of the piano; today she even began to cry, when I began to play. In general I think she is remarkably free from fear or shyness of any sort. She goes to anyone who will take her. Staring at strangers to be sure, and being very grave when they are in the room, but not crying, or clinging to me. I am very glad of this, as though it is very flattering and endearing to me, yet I should be sorry if she were to get the habit of refusing to go to others.

Then as to her 'bodily' qualifications, she has two teeth cut with very little trouble; but I believe the worst are to come. She is very strong in her limbs, though because she is so fat, we do not let her use her ancles at all, and I hope she will be rather late in walking that her little legs may be very firm. I shall find it difficult to damp the energies of the servants in this respect, but I intend that she shall teach herself to walk, & receive no assistance from hands &c. She lies down on the floor a good deal, and kicks about; a practice I began very early, and which has done her a great deal of good. She goes to bed *awake*; another practice I began early, and which is so comfortable I wonder it is not more generally adopted. Once or twice we have had grand cryings, which have been very very distressing to me; but when I have convinced myself that she is not in pain, is perfectly well, and that she is only wanting to be taken up I have been quite firm, though I have sometimes cried almost as much as she has. I never leave her till she is asleep (except in extreme cases) and as she is put to bed at a regular time (6 o'clock) she generally gets very sleepy while being undressed. While the undressing is going on, I never like her to be talked to, played with, or excited yet sometimes she is so very playful when she ought to be put down, that a turn or two up and down the room is required to soothe her, still putting her down awake. Sometimes she will cry a little, and when I turn her over in her cot she fancies she is going to be taken up and is still in a moment making the peculiar little triumphing noise she does when she is pleased.

Crying has been a great difficulty with me. Books do so differ. One says 'Do not let them have anything they cry for', another (Mme Neckar de Saussure, sur L'Education Progressive, the nicest book I have read on the subject) says 'les larmes des enfans [*sic*] sont si amères, la calme parfaite . . .'

For more from Mrs Gaskell, her fourth novel, *North and South*, is to be highly recommended: though not as well known as *Cranford*, it is far more gripping.

CHOKING

IT is always advisable regularly to remind oneself of first aid techniques such as what to do when a baby chokes, if only to reassure worried grandparents as one embarks upon a stint of Baby-Led Weaning. So here is what to do for babies up to the age of one.

1. If the baby is unable to breathe, cough or cry and you suspect that they have a severe obstruction in their throat, give back blows.
    - Lay the baby face down along your forearm with his head lower than his bottom.
    - Give up to five back blows between the baby's shoulder blades with the heel of your hand.
    - After each blow, check the baby's mouth, turning him face up along your other forearm and supporting the back and head. Pick out any obvious instructions.
    - Effective back blows cure the majority of choking incidents.

2. If the baby is still choking, give chest thrusts.
    - Place two fingertips on the lower half of the baby's breast-bone, a finger's breadth below the nipples.
    - Give up to five sharp thrusts, pushing inwards and towards the head. After each thrust, re-check the mouth.

3. If the baby is still choking after three full cycles of back blows and chest thrusts, call an ambulance.
    - Repeat cycles of back blows and chest thrusts until medical help arrives.
    - If the baby loses consciousness, give CPR.
    - Seek medical advice for any baby who has been given chest thrusts as there is a risk of internal damage.
    - For anyone older than a year a different technique is used; see redcross.org/firstaid.

Source: British Red Cross

WHAT TO DO IF YOU RUN OUT OF NAPPIES

NAPPIES used to be called 'diapers', from a Middle English word that referred to a type of cotton or linen cloth with a diamond pattern on it that was used to keep a baby dry. While the word stuck in America, in Britain it was gradually replaced in common parlance by 'nappy', which is a derivation of 'napkin'. Nursemaids used pins or ties to secure nappies, or sometimes even stitched the baby in with a needle and thread, which made sense in the pre-twentieth century era when nappies were usually only changed twice or thrice a day.

Sometimes, however, unfortunate circumstances require a return to those days: your plane is held on the runway for several hours, or you get stranded on top of a mountain, or you find yourself in the midst of an alien invasion, or you are unexpectedly invited to stay an extra day aboard David Geffen's yacht as it cruises around the Caribbean, or you are simply too lazy or drunk to go to the shops to buy more disposables ones or to the sink to wash more cloth ones. But do not panic. Just follow these simple instructions.

1. Get hold of a piece of cloth of some sort – for example, a napkin, headscarf, T-shirt, towel, tea towel or flag.
2. Fold the piece of cloth to the width of the baby's waist.
3. Lay the folded cloth down vertically, ideally on a flat surface covered by something softish such as grass.
4. Place the baby on his (or her) back on the cloth.
5. Take the bottom half of the piece of cloth and bring it between the baby's legs and up to his waist. Then twist it round 180 degrees and fold the two front corners in.

6. Use safety pins to secure the two back corners to the front of what is now the baby's nappy – though if you are the type of mother who carries safety pins, you are probably not the type of mother who runs out of nappies. Alternatives to safety pins include hair clips, binder clips from the office, etc. If really desperate, use tape to secure the nappy snugly around the waist and at the legs. Or track down a needle and thread and then stitch the baby in: see above.

THE OLD FIRE

EVERYONE changes when they have a baby. 'The old fire' is how Tolstoy characterized one of the aspects of a woman that, once she becomes a mother, tends to get submerged under a pile of nappies, even if only for a little while. Tolstoy knew what he was talking about: his wife, Sonya, who copied out every single word of *War and Peace* by hand for her husband, also bore him thirteen children. It is worth trying to reignite that fire occasionally, however, not least because Tolstoy writes of Natasha in *War and Peace*: 'At the rare moments when the old fire did kindle in her handsome, fully developed body she was even more attractive than in former days.' So here, to help you tap into your pre-baby self that led you regularly to dance on tabletops in Lycra dresses of a Saturday night, is a list of every Madonna song ever released in the UK.

Year	Song	Highest chart position
1984	'Holiday'	6
	'Lucky Star'	14
	'Borderline'	56
	'Like a Virgin'	3
1985	'Material Girl'	3
	'Crazy for You'	2
	'Into the Groove'	1
	'Holiday' (again)	2
	'Angel'	5
	'Gambler'	4
	'Dress You Up'	5
1986	'Borderline' (again)	2
	'Live to Tell'	2
	'Lucky Star' (again)	83
	'Papa Don't Preach'	1
	'True Blue'	1
	'Open Your Heart'	4
1987	'La Isla Bonita'	1
	'Who's That Girl?'	1
	'Causing a Commotion'	4
	'The Look of Love'	9
1988	–	–
1989	'Like a Prayer'	1
	'Into the Groove'/'Who's That Girl?'	99
	'Express Yourself'	5
	'Cherish'	3
	'Dear Jessie'	5
1990	'Vogue'	1
	'Hanky Panky'	2
	'Justify My Love'	2
1991	'Crazy for You' (again)	2
	'Rescue Me'	3
	'Holiday' (again)	5
1992	'This Used to Be My Playground'	3
	'Erotica'	3
	'Deeper and Deeper'	6
1993	'Bad Girl'	10
	'Fever'	6
	'Rain'	7
1994	'I'll Remember'	7
	'Secret'	5
	'Take a Bow'	16

Year	Song	Highest chart position
1995	'Bedtime Story'	4
	'Human Nature'	8
	'You'll See'	5
1996	'Oh Father'	16
	'One More Chance'	11
	'You Must Love Me'	10
	'Don't Cry for Me Argentina'	3
1997	'Another Suitcase in Another Hall'	7
1998	'Frozen'	1
	'Ray of Light'	2
	'Drowned World'/'Substitute for Love'	10
	'The Power of Good-Bye'/'Little Star'	6
1999	'Nothing Really Matters'	7
	'Beautiful Stranger'	2
2000	'American Pie'	1
	'Music'	1
	'Don't Tell Me'	4
2001	'What It Feels Like for a Girl'	7
2002	'Die Another Day'	3
2003	'American Life'	2
	'Hollywood'	2
	'Love Profusion'	11
2005	'Hung Up'	1
2006	'Sorry'	1
	'Get Together'	7
	'Jump'	9
2007	–	–
2008	'4 Minutes'	1
	'Give It 2 Me'	7
	'Miles Away'	39
2009	'Celebration'	3

Many a pub quiz has been clinched with the correct answer to 'What was Madonna's first UK single?' Answer: 'Holiday', *not* 'Lucky Star', as often thought. 'Into the Groove' was, however, her first UK number one.

WORRY

ONE of the most surprising aspects of Virginia Woolf's diaries is the amount of time she spends worrying about clothes. Worry worry worry — it's a very modern affliction. And worry levels increase stratospherically the minute a baby is born. Flat head syndrome? Honey causes botulism? Forward-facing buggies? Rear-facing car seats? Lead poisoning from eating earth? The gold-plated pram or the diamond-encrusted sling? Compared to our own car-seat-less, let-them-eat-dirt, smoking and drinking mothers, life has in recent years become inexorably more complicated, in a world where seemingly every day the media trumpets about some new way to endanger our baby that had thus far not even occurred to us.

But what almost every experienced mother will tell you once they emerge from the fog of the baby years is that, if they regret anything, it is that they wish they had worried less and enjoyed more. The question, then, is how this is to be achieved. The foremost experts on worry are Americans, many of whom (with apologies for the sweeping generalization, but) seem to exist in a near-permanent state of fear. '[T]hey are so mad and ill and frightened,' Nancy Mitford observed of our transatlantic cousins in *Don't Tell Alfred* (1960), one of her (dare one say it?) marginally less heavenly books. Anyone who has ever spent time in an American playground will concur that it is simply extraordinary the things American parents find to worry about. No wonder, then, that much of the relevant self-help literature also comes from that side of the pond. The classic of the genre is *How to Stop Worrying and Start Living* (1948) by Dale Carnegie, and there have been numerous imitators since.

Self-help books, however, clearly do not work, because if they did they would no longer exist. So instead, let us turn to another American voice, that of F. Scott Fitzgerald. He is not often praised for his parenting prowess, but consider making an exception just this once. Here is an extract from a letter he wrote to his daughter Scottie on 8 August 1933:

Things to worry about:

Worry about courage
Worry about cleanliness
Worry about efficiency
Worry about horsemanship
Worry about . . .

Things not to worry about:

Don't worry about popular opinion
Don't worry about dolls
Don't worry about the past
Don't worry about the future
Don't worry about growing up
Don't worry about anybody getting ahead of you
Don't worry about triumph
Don't worry about failure unless it comes through your own
   fault
Don't worry about mosquitoes
Don't worry about flies
Don't worry about insects in general
Don't worry about parents
Don't worry about boys
Don't worry about disappointments

Don't worry about pleasures
Don't worry about satisfactions

Things to think about:

What am I really aiming at?

It is this final line of Fitzgerald's merry scribblings that holds the key: 'What am I really aiming at?' In other words, consider your long-term goals, rather than your short-term ones. Which in actual fact is excellent advice when it comes to parenting generally.

WHAT WE BUY

Product	UK retail value (2004)	UK retail value (2009)	Increase in value over the last five years
Infant clothing	£1,057.9m	£1,174.7m	11 per cent
Nappies	£468.5m	£470.1m	0.3 per cent
Baby wipes	£184.4m	£216.5m	17.4 per cent
Baby toiletries	£44.2m	£53.3m	20.7 per cent
Baby hair care	£17.7m	£18.5m	5 per cent
Baby skin care	£26m	£30.6m	17.7 per cent
Baby sun care	£22.5m	£26.6m	18.3 per cent
Milk formula	£201.4m	£270.9m	34.5 per cent
Baby food: prepared	£116.8m	£158.4m	35.7 per cent
Baby food: dried	£30.1m	£30.6m	1.7 per cent
Infant toys	£211.6m	£300.7m	42.1 per cent

Source: Euromonitor International

HOW TO MAKE FIRE

HAVING a baby really makes one think about one's cave-woman predecessors: how the dickens did they manage without all the many inventions — a self-pushing buggy that also simultaneously sterilizes bottles and increases IQ, say — that these days seem to be deemed essential accoutrements for every modern mother? But miraculously, they did. And so let us honour them by getting in touch with the cave-woman inside all of us — no, not by slaughtering a dinosaur with our bare hands, but rather by learning how to make fire. It is one of the most basic of survival skills, and with mastering it also comes the knowledge that, should some sort of apocalyptic disaster strike, you will always have the essentials of light and heat with which to see and warm your baby. Plus, the light of a flickering fire is so wonderfully flattering. Those cavewomen were on to something, it turns out.

First, gather some tinder: grass, leaves, tree bark, paper, anything as long as it is dry and therefore catches fire easily. Also bear in mind that dark-coloured tinder absorbs heat and light more effectively than light-coloured tinder.

Then choose a spot to make your fire that is protected from the wind. Clear away any debris, and arrange your tinder in a pile either on solid ground or on a layer of stones. This will help ensure that the fire does not spread out of control.

The easiest way to make fire requires you first to track down a pair of specs, some binoculars or a magnifying glass. Sprinkle a little bit of water on the lens (this intensifies the beam), and then angle it towards the sun to create a beam of sunlight that shines through the lens and hits the tinder. Hold it there until you see sparks, and eventually a flame.

If there is no sunlight (if, say, dark clouds have gathered or night has fallen), making fire becomes a tad more challenging. One frequently used method creates fire from friction and is known as the 'hand drill' method, but it demands a huge amount of practice and is physically very hard work, especially if you also have a screaming baby to contend with. So instead, let us turn to the 'flint and metal' method, which was used at least as far back as the Neolithic age 4,000–10,000 years ago.

First get hold of a piece of metal that contains iron: pyrite, marcasite or, more common in everyday life, steel in the form of a steel knife. You will then need to pair this with any kind of very hard rock that fractures to a sharp edge: flint is ideal and most commonly used, but quartz, jade or agate will also do. It is not the flint itself that produces the sparks, but rather the way that striking it releases small particles of iron which, when exposed to the oxygen in the air, make fire.

Pile of tinder in place, use the steel knife to strike repeatedly downwards on the flint in quick, short strokes, aiming any resulting sparks at the tinder. Always strike away from your body. As soon as you see sparks fall on the tinder (hopefully within about fifteen seconds, but it takes a little bit of practice), blow gently on them to transform them into flames.

Tah-dah!

THE ORIGINS OF WORDS

Baby

Originally 'baban', then 'babe', then 'baby'. According to the *Oxford English Dictionary*, the earliest written reference is found in the 1377 version of William Langland's *Piers Plowman*.

Mother

Derived from the Old English word *modor*, which itself comes from an Indo-European root (c.f. the Latin term *mater* and the Greek term *meter*). More colloquial forms like 'mama', 'mammy' or 'mummy' imitate 'early infantile vocalisation' as the *OED* grandly calls it – that is, a baby's first attempts to communicate.

Pregnant

From the Latin word *praegnant*, which was formed from the preposition *prae*, meaning 'before', and the base of the verb *gnasci*, meaning 'be born'.

Birth

From the Old Norse word *byrth*. A Viking import, then.

Babysitter

A 1930s import from America.

Cry

A Middle English word that originally meant 'to ask for loudly'. Derived from the Old French verb *crier*, which in turn is from the Latin *quiritare*, meaning 'to raise a public outcry' — which, when your baby is bawling in the supermarket, is exactly right.

Tired

The first written use of the word comes in a poem about the Scottish hero Sir William Wallace, written in 1470 by Henry the Minstrel (who sounds like a character from a Monty Python film, but was actually a real person, amazingly, who also went by the equally brilliant name of Blind Harry).

Grumpy

The origin is unclear, but may be the Danish word *grum*, meaning 'cruel'. It was first used in Fanny Burney's best-selling novel of 1778, *Evelina*: 'You were so grumpy you would not let me.'

Help

An Old English word which first appeared in print in a 1552 version of the ancient epic poem *Beowulf*.

Chocolate (useful if the above is not available)

'The chiefe use of this Cacao is in a drinke which they call Chocolate' is the first written reference to the word, according to the *OED*, in a 1604 translation of Joseph D'Acosta's *History of the Indies* by D'Acosta. It originally comes from a word in Nahuatl, the language spoken in central Mexico by the Aztecs, which also gave us 'avocado' and 'chilli'.

TOP FIVE TIPS FOR A FABULOUS FIRST BIRTHDAY PARTY

HURRAH! You made it through the first year. Your child is still in one piece, you've managed to keep him or her alive and fed and sheltered with no discernible (physical) scars for life — 'tis quite an achievement. It is you who ought to get all the presents, really. Alternatively, pat yourself on the back, reach for a cocktail and take on board these top tips to make sure that the first birthday party is a rip-roaring rampage of fun for all concerned.

1. *Timing*

Do not schedule the party on the same day as the actual birthday. You'll spend the whole day blowing up balloons and making cucumber sandwiches, when all you want to do is be mucking around with your little one. On the invitation (emailed or otherwise), give a start time *and* an end time that works with their nap schedule — for example, 3.00–5.00 p.m.; otherwise you'll find the guests without children are still hanging around hoping to be offered another drink at 6.00 p.m. when clearly it is bath time.

2. *The guest list*

Do not invite too many people. There really ought to be a law against having more than five small children in one's house at any one time, a state of affairs which results in (at best) one feeling like a waiter in a zoo, rather than the proud parent of a one-year-old. Far more sensible is to invite two or three friends who have babies of a similar age round for tea or out for a picnic (weather permitting). Depending on the number of celebrities who will be attending, and hence the number of paparazzi, consider valet parking, a marquee and some heavies. Whatever you do, do not threaten to call the police on the paparazzi, since they have heard this one many times before, and it only makes for better headlines: 'POLICE CALLED AS KID'S PARTY DESCENDS INTO CHAOS TERROR'.

3. The decorations

It is nigh impossible to have too many balloons: stick to just one or two colours, and be warned that (who knew?) they burst when exposed to strong direct sunlight. As for the food table, it is very easy to make the decorations yourself, perhaps themed according to your child's current favourite book. *Peter Rabbit*, say: 'First he ate some radishes, and then he ate some French beans.'

Or *The Very Hungry Caterpillar*: 'On Friday he ate through five oranges, but he was still hungry.'

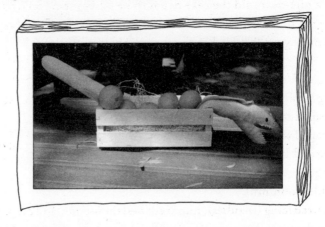

To be truly chic, the choice of font is crucial: Courier perhaps? Anything as long as it is not Comic Sans, which is the font of all evil. It ought to be a crime to use Comic Sans. In the more tasteful countries – France, say – it probably is.

4. The child

There are a number of laws regarding how the child will behave at his or her first birthday party. Make sure your child is made aware of them, and accept them yourself with Zen-like calm. They are: a) the child will, the day before, develop some sort of mild illness like a cold, cough or ear infection; b) the child will get food on his or her sweet (and probably new) little outfit within thirty seconds of donning it; and c) the child will cry when the cake is brought out, candles a-blazing, cameras a-snapping. Which brings us to . . .

5. The cake

For a one-year-old the cake needs to be fairly plain. So here is a recipe that even the most domestically challenged among us can manage.

170g self-raising flour
170g sugar
1 heaped tablespoon cocoa powder
1 heaped teaspoon baking powder
170g soft butter
3 eggs
1 tablespoon milk
coloured icing (in tubes), hundreds and thousands, and candles,
   to decorate

For the icing:
75g butter
100g brown sugar
150g icing sugar
50g cocoa powder

The butter must be soft, so leave it out at room temperature for a few hours. If you forget, mash it up with a fork first, or microwave for a few seconds.

Preheat the oven to 170°C/325°F/Gas Mark 3.

Ready the cake tins – ideally two 18cm (7in) round tins cake tins at least 4cm (1 in) deep, if you want to put icing in the middle, but any shape is fine. Butter the sides and line the bottom with greaseproof paper. (To do this, draw round the base on to paper, cut it out and butter the tin to stick it down. But check the box: some greaseproof paper needs buttering, some is non-stick.)

Put the flour, sugar, cocoa powder and baking powder in a bowl. Add the butter, eggs and milk, and mix well with a wooden spoon or fork until creamy. This will take 2–3 minutes. Or you can use a food mixer. The mixture should fall easily off a spoon. Add a little more milk if it is too thick.

Divide the mixture between the baking tins and smooth the surface with a spoon. Cook for 20–30 minutes. Test if it is cooked by pressing the top with your finger. The cake should spring back; if your finger leaves a dent, it needs longer. Leave the cakes to cool for a few minutes in the tin, and then turn them out. Cool on a wire cooling rack if you have one, or balance over the tin (letting the air circulate stops the base going soggy).

Meanwhile, make the icing. In a saucepan melt the butter with two tablespoons of water and the brown sugar. Bring to the boil and immediately stir in the icing sugar and the cocoa power. Beat till smooth. Let it cool. Then sandwich the cakes together with the icing in between and on top.

The difficult bit is the decorating: it requires true artistic skill to squeeze the coloured icing out of the tube just so, and add the perfect amount of hundreds and thousands. Don't forget a single, splendid candle too.

Come the morning after, sweep up those cake crumbs, write those thank-you cards (just a postcard, not a letter, please: a letter suggests to its recipients that you have a suspicious amount of time on your hands for a newish mother) and, lo!, let the conversations about if/when to have another baby begin.

FERTILITY RATES AROUND THE WORLD

Average number of children per woman in countries listed alphabetically from N to Z only

Namibia	3.4	Sierra Leone	5.2
Nauru	3.3	Singapore	1.3
Nepal	2.9	Slovakia	1.3
Netherlands	1.7	Slovenia	1.4
Netherlands Antilles	2.0	Solomon Islands	3.9
New Caledonia	2.1	Somalia	6.4
New Zealand	2.0	South Africa	2.6
Nicaragua	2.8	Spain	1.4
Nieu	2.6	Sri Lanka	2.3
Niger	7.1	Sudan	4.2
Nigeria	5.3	Suriname	2.4
Northern Mariana Islands	1.6	Swaziland	3.6
Norway	1.9	Sweden	1.9
Occupied Palestinian Territory	5.1	Switzerland	1.5
Oman	3.1	Syrian Arab Republic	3.3
Oz (Australia)	1.9	Tajikistan	3.5
Pakistan	4.0	TFYR of Macedonia	1.4
Palau	2.0	Thailand	1.8
Panama	2.6	Timor–Leste	6.5
Papua New Guinea	4.1	Togo	4.3
Paraguay	3.1	Trinidad and Tobago	1.6
Peru	2.6	Tunisia	1.9
Philippines	3.1	Turkey	2.1
Poland	1.3	Turkmenistan	2.5
Portugal	1.4	Tuvalu	3.7
Puerto Rico	1.8	Uganda	6.4
Qatar	2.4	Ukraine	1.3
Republic of Korea	1.2	United Arab Emirates	1.9
Republic of Moldova	1.5	United Kingdom	1.8
Reunion	2.4	United Republic of Tanzania	5.6
Romania	1.3	United States of America	2.1
Russian Federation	1.4	United States Virgin Islands	2.1
Rwanda	5.4	Uruguay	2.1
Saint Lucia	2.0	Uzbekistan	2.3
Saint Vincent and the Grenadines	2.1	Vanuatu	4.0
Samoa	4.0	Venezuela	2.5
San Marino	1.3	Vietnam	2.1
Sao Tome and Principe	3.9	Wallis and Futuna Islands	2.0
Saudi Arabia	3.2	Western Sahara	2.7
Senegal	5.0	Yemen	5.3
Serbia	1.6	Zambia	5.9
Seychelles	2.2	Zimbabwe	3.5

Source: United Nations Department of Economic and Social Affairs

ACKNOWLEDGEMENTS

Thanks to Helen Garnons-Williams, Erica Jarnes, Heather Goldstein and everyone at Bloomsbury, Clare Conville, Chris and Nicola Beauman, David and Susan Bobin, Olivia Lacey, Jennie Cox, Jennifer Wilkinson, Corinna Csaky and most of all to James, Madelaine and Jack Bobin.

PERMISSIONS

The table of information on pages 15–24 is from the Statistics and Indicators on Women and Men database © United Nations 2010. Reproduced with permission.

The list of hotels on pages 30–31 is copyright © 2003 Condé Nast Publications. All rights reserved. Originally published on www.concierge.com. Reprinted by permission.

The table on information on pages 37–41 is reprinted by permission of the Marine Conservation Society UK.

The extract on pages 54–55 is from *Kamasutra*, edited by Wendy Doniger and Sudhir Kakar, copyright © OWC, 2009. Reprinted by permission of Oxford University Press.

The table on page 69 is reproduced under the terms of the Click-Use Licence.

A NOTE ON FRANCESCA BEAUMAN

FRANCESCA Beauman graduated from Cambridge University with a first class degree in History. She is the author of *The Pineapple: King of Fruits*, *The Woman's Book: Everything but the Kitchen Sink* and *Shapely Ankle Preferr'd: A History of the Lonely Hearts Ad*. She also writes and presents for television. She divides her time between London and Los Angeles and is married with two young children.

A NOTE ON MRS EAVES

MRS Eaves is a transitional serif typeface designed by Zuzana Licko in 1996, and licensed by Emigre, a typefoundry run by Licko and her husband Rudy VanderLans. Mrs Eaves is a revival of a 1757 type designed by English printer John Baskerville, and is related to contemporary Baskerville typefaces.

Like Baskerville, Mrs Eaves has a near-vertical stress. Identifying characters include the lowercase g with its open lower counter and swash-like ear; the uppercase Q with its flowing swash-like tail; the uppercase C with its serifs at top and bottom; and the uppercase G with its sharp spur suggesting a vestigial serif.

Mrs Eaves is named after Sarah Eaves, who was Baskerville's housekeeper. When she and her five children were abandoned by Mr Eaves, she and Baskerville got together, working side by side and eventually marrying when the estranged husband died. Like the widows of Caslon, Bodoni, and the daughters of Fournier, Sarah completed the printing of the unfinished volumes that John Baskerville left upon his death. The name 'Mrs Eaves' honours one of the forgotten mothers in the history of typography.